Blessings *of* Heaven

TIMELESS WISDOM
and
SPIRITUAL TRUTHS

Compiled by Stephen Hines

THOMAS NELSON
Since 1798

NASHVILLE   MEXICO CITY   RIO DE JANEIRO

Published in Nashville, Tennessee, by Thomas Nelson. Thomas Nelson is a registered trademark of HarperCollins Christian Publishing.

Thomas Nelson titles may be purchased in bulk for educational, business, fund-raising, or sales promotional use. For information, please e-mail SpecialMarket@ThomasNelson.com.

All Scripture quotations, unless otherwise indicated, are taken from The New King James Version. © 1982 by Thomas Nelson. Used by permission. All rights reserved.

Many Scriptural references by nineteenth and early twentieth century writers are from the King James Version of the Bible.

Other Scripture references are from the following sources: THE ENGLISH STANDARD VERSION. © 2001 by Crossway Bibles, a division of Good News Publishers. Used by permission. NEW AMERICAN STANDARD BIBLE®. © The Lockman Foundation 1960,1962, 1963, 1968, 1971, 1972, 1975, 1977, 1995. Used by permission. Scripture quotations marked NIV are taken from the Holy Bible, New International Version®, NIV® Copyright © 1973, 1978, 1984, 2011 by Biblica, Inc.™ Used by permission of Zondervan. All rights reserved worldwide. www.zondervan.com.

Grateful acknowledgment is made to the following for permission to reprint material copyrighted or controlled by them:

Mere Christianity by C. S. Lewis copyright © C. S. Lewis Pte. Ltd. 1942, 1943, 1944, 1952. Extracts reprinted by permission.

A Brief History of Heaven by Alister E. McGrath. Copyright © 2003 by Alister E. McGrath. Published by Blackwell Publishing Ltd. Used by permission.

The Glory of Heaven: The Truth About Heaven, Angels, and Eternal Life (Second Edition) by John MacArthur © 1996, 2013 by John MacArthur, pp. 146-151. Used by permission of Crossway, a publishing ministry of Good News Publishers, Wheaton, Il 60187, www.crossway.org.

What Happens After I Die? by Michael Allen Rogers © 2013 by Michael Allen Rogers, Kindle edition. Used by permission of Crossway, a publishing ministry of Good News Publishers, Wheaton, Il 60187, www.crossway.org.

The Hope of Glory by Dale Moody © 1964 by Dale Moody. Published by Wm. B. Eerdmans Publishing Company. Reprinted by permission of the publisher. All rights reserved.

Library of Congress Cataloging-in-Publication Data

ISBN 978-0-7180-3209-8

Printed in the United States of America

1 2 3 4 5 DCI 1 8 17 16 15 14

TABLE OF CONTENTS

Introduction to *Blessings of Heaven*. 9

When I Die, Will I Go Immediately to Heaven or Not? 11

Will I Feel at Home in Heaven? 16

Is My Wanting to Go to Heaven Merely a Hope for
   "Pie in the Sky By and By"? 19

How Can Reflecting on Heaven Help Me Escape the
   "Tyranny of the Urgent"? 22

Do Those Now in Heaven Have Any Interest in Us? 26

Will We Be Satisfied with Heaven? 29

Will I Be the Same Person in Heaven That I Now Am
   on Earth? 33

Does My Heavenly Home Have a Location? 37

What Will It Be Like to Have a Perfect Body? 43

How Can Thoughts of Heaven Comfort Me in My Trials
   and Help Me Achieve Peace of Heart? 48

How Can I Be Sure I Will Go to Heaven? .53

What Am I to Make of Some Special Revelation of the Lord
   That Is Precious to Me But Is Not Manifested in Scripture? 57

Will Children Enjoy Heaven? 62

Will Being in Heaven Help Me Find Out Who I Am
   As a Person? 67

What Will It Be Like to Be Free from the Temptation to Sin? 70

How Can I Enjoy a Taste of Heaven in My Everyday Walk? 74

Do We Long for God's Heavenly Rewards? 78

How May I Receive the Gift of Heaven in a Way
   That Pleases Him? 81

What Can I Do to Bring a Touch of Heaven to Earth? 85

How Does the Allegory of Sarah and Hagar Reveal Aspects
   of Heaven? 89

How Does God's Witness in Nature Suggest the Reality
   of Heaven? 92

Is My Longing for Heaven a Clue That Heaven
   Is Really There? 96

How Do the Heavens Declare the Glory of God? 99

How Can I Explain Heaven to My Children? 103

How Are the Different Meanings for the Word "Heaven"
   Explained in the Bible? 107

Have You Ever Thought of Death As a Gift? 111

Will My Pet Go to Heaven? 114

What Taste of Heaven Now Hints of the Life to Come? 118

Are the New Heaven and the New Earth Mentioned in
   Places Other Than the Book of Revelation? 123

Will Heaven Be Big Enough to Hold Everyone? 127

Can the Promise of Heaven Be Used As an Evangelistic Tool? 132

Won't We Be Jealous If Others Receive Greater Rewards
   in Heaven Than We Do? 135

Can an Illness Draw Us Closer to Heaven? 140

Is There Any Good Reason for Believing in Life After Death? 144

What's Important in Heaven: the Quality or Quantity
   of My Works? 148

If Life Itself Has Been a Struggle, Will Eternal Life Be
   Any Better? 152

Will Our Souls Fall Asleep Until the Resurrection
   of the Dead? 156

Have You Ever Felt the Stirring of God's Heavenly Spirit? 160

How Can We Encourage Others on Their Journey
   to Heaven? 163

How Do the Angels of Heaven Act for Us Now on Earth? 167

What Does the Symbolic Language of Heaven
   Tell Us About Jesus? 170

Does Having a Heavenly Treasure in Earthen Vessels
   Dim Our View of the Future? 174

Do We Deserve the Gift of Heaven? 179

What Are We to Make of "Near Death" Experiences? 183

Will Our Heavenly Bodies Be Real or Immaterial? 186

How Will Heaven Be Similar to Life Now? 190

What Can a Child Teach Us About Heaven? 194

What Can the Sermon on the Mount Tell Us
   About Heaven? 198

Is There Any Heavenly Good in Keeping Score
   of Good Deeds? 202

How Old Will We Be in Heaven? 206

BLESSINGS OF HEAVEN

Stephen Hines

Christians are at their best when they are looking ahead.

The early church converted much of the known world to Christ because of a vital belief in the resurrection of Christ from the dead and in their own resurrection at the last day. The church awoke from its medieval torpor when the monk Martin Luther reintroduced the concepts of salvation by grace and of having a personal relationship with God not mediated by men. And the great revivals of the eighteenth and nineteenth centuries were driven in large measure by a renewed vision of the second coming of the Lord to establish his kingdom on earth.

Now, in our own time, we are being renewed by the words of those who testify to the reality of our heavenly home and the glory of what awaits us when we enter Jesus' presence.

For twenty or thirty years now we have had a rich treasury of reminders that the loss of our loved ones does not leave us grieving without hope. This devotional book, *Blessings of Heaven*, is one more reminder that our Lord is forever with us, giving us a taste of heaven now and a real heaven in the life to come.

Writers as diverse as Augustine, Chuck Swindoll, John Wesley, Joni Eareckson Tada, C. S. Lewis, Randy Alcorn, and Anne Graham Lotz reflect on what heaven means to them, and the reader is encouraged to do likewise.

There are questions to be asked, meditations to be considered, and answers to be acted on in the following pages.

As you read, think, and apply what you learn, may you be drawn up into heavenly places in Christ Jesus (see Eph. 1:3).

When I Die, Will I Go Immediately to Heaven or Not?

D. L. Moody (1837–1899)

D. L. Moody, America's most famous evangelist of the nineteenth century, illuminates the biblical order of life after death in this sermon titled, "Heavenly Inhabitants." In attitude and tone, these words wonderfully characterize the man who founded Moody Bible Institute, Moody Church in Chicago, and Moody Publishers. It should be noted that there have always been a great many differences of opinion as to how all the elements of the afterlife are related to one another. As you read Moody, keep in mind that not all of the writers who follow him will necessarily take his line of thought. Yet as we expose ourselves to different views about our eternal home, let us hope we will be inspired by the wonder, the mystery, and the possibilities of the place God has prepared for us. This selection is taken from Moody's book *Heaven: Where It Is, Its Inhabitants, and How to Get There,* published by Fleming Revell in 1885.

We Will Live Forever

It says in the 12th chapter of John and the 26th verse: "If any man serve me, let him follow me; and where I am, there shall also my servant be."

I cannot agree with some people, that Paul has been sleeping in the grave, and is still there, after the storms of eighteen hundred years. I cannot believe that he who loved the Master, who had such a burning zeal for Him, has been separated from Him in an unconscious state, "Father, I will that they also, whom thou hast given me, be with me where I am; that they may behold my glory, which thou has given me." [John 17:24] This is Christ's prayer.

Now when a man believes on the Lord Jesus Christ, he gets eternal life. A great many people make a mistake right there: "He that believeth on the Son hath—h-a-t-h—hath eternal life;" [John 3:36] it does not say he shall have it when he comes to die; it is in the present tense; it is mine now—if I believe. It is the gift of God, that is enough. You can't bury the gift of God; you can't buy eternal life. All the grave-diggers in the world can't dig a grave large enough and deep enough to hold eternal life; all the coffin-makers in the world can't make a coffin large enough and strong enough to hold eternal life; it is mine; it is mine!

I believe when Paul said "To be absent from the body and present with the Lord," [2 Cor. 5:8] he meant what he said; that he was not going to be separated from Him for eighteen hundred years; that spirit that he got when he was converted he got from a new life and a new nature, and they could not lay that away in the sepulcher; they could not bury it that flew to meet its Maker. It may be he is not satisfied, and will not be until the resurrection, but Christ says: "He will see then the travail of his soul, and be satisfied." [Isa. 53:11] Even the body shall be raised; this body, sown in dishonor, shall be raised in glory; this body which has put on corruption, shall put on incorruption, and this mortal shall put on immortality. It is only a question of time. The great morning of the world will, by-and-by, dawn upon the earth, and the dead shall come forth and shall hear the voice of Him who is the resurrection and the life.

Paul says: "If our earthly house of this tabernacle were dissolved, we have a building of God, an house not made with hands, eternal in the heavens." [2 Cor. 5:1] He could take down the clay temple, and leave that, but he had a better house. He says in one place: I am in a strait betwixt two; having a desire to depart and be with Christ, which is far better; nevertheless to abide in the flesh is more needful for me. [Phil. 1:23-24] To me, it is a sweet thought to think that death does not separate us from the Master. A great many people are living continually in the bondage of death, but if I have eternal life, death cannot touch that; it may touch the house I live in; it may change my countenance and send my body away to the grave, but it cannot touch this new life. To me it is very sad to think that so many professed Christians look upon death as they do.

I received some time ago a letter from a friend in London, and I thought, as I read it, I would take it and read it to other people and see if I could not get them to look upon death as this friend does. He lost a loved mother. In England it is a very common thing to send out cards in memory of the departed ones, and they put upon them great borders of black—sometimes a quarter of an inch of black border—but this friend has gone and put on gold; he did not put on black at all; she had gone to the golden city, and so he just put on a golden border; and I think it is a good deal better than black. I think when our friends die, instead of putting a great black border upon our memorials to make them look dark, it would be better for us to put on gold.

It is not death at all; it is life. Someone said to a person dying; "Well, you are in the land of the living yet." "No," said he, "I am in the land of the dying yet, but I am going to the land of the living; they live there and never die." This is the land of sin and death and tears, but up yonder they never die. It is perpetual life; it is unceasing joy.

"It is a glorious thing to die," was the testimony of Hannah Moore on her deathbed, though her life had been sown thick with the rarest friendships, and age had not so weakened her memory as to cause her to forget those little hamlets among the cliffs of her native hills, or the mission-schools she had with such perseverance established, and where she would be so sadly missed.

As James Montgomery has said:

> "There is a soft, a down bed;
> 'Tis fair as breath of even;
> A couch for weary mortals spread,
> Where they may rest the aching head,
> And find repose—in heaven!
>
> "There is an hour of peaceful rest,
> To mourning wanderers given.
> There is a joy for souls distressed
> A balm for every wounded breast,
> 'Tis found alone—in heaven!"

---

*W*orth Thinking About

Moody has made his case. What do you think of it? Is it how you have been taught or the way you think about "being absent from the body and present with the Lord"? Or does it really make any difference as to manners and modes and ways of entering eternity? Do you look forward to the resurrection of the dead with the same zeal as you look forward to being in heaven?

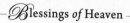

WHEN THE ROLL IS CALLED UP YONDER

When the trumpet of the Lord shall sound,
and time shall be no more,
And the morning breaks eternal, bright and fair,
When the saved of earth shall gather over on the other shore,
And the roll is called up yonder, I'll be there. . . .
Let us labor for the Master from the dawn to setting sun,
Let us talk of all His wondrous love and care;
Then when all of life is over, and our work on earth is done,
And the roll is called up yonder, I'll be there.

—J. M. Black

rayer

DEAR FATHER, THANK YOU FOR YOUR PROMISES OF ETERNAL LIFE NOW AND THE EVEN GREATER EXPERIENCE OF LIFE ETERNAL IN THE WORLD TO COME. HELP US TO REALIZE THAT DEATH DOES NOT HAVE THE STING IT HAD BEFORE CHRIST CAME, FOR NOW IT ENTERS US INTO HIS PRESENCE. AMEN.

WILL I FEEL AT HOME IN HEAVEN?

Anne Graham Lotz

Perhaps your own home life was not what you thought it should have been, and this makes it difficult for you to think of heaven in positive terms at all. It is hard to want a home in heaven if you are not sure what a good home is. Anne Graham Lotz, daughter of evangelist Billy Graham, and founder of AnGel Ministries, offers some reassuring words about the home life to be found in heaven in her book, *Heaven: My Father's House,* Thomas Nelson Publishers, 2001. Let us not be afraid that heaven will not match up with our hopes but that we will feel loved and absolutely accepted as we are. The home for which we have always yearned will have been found.

What is the home of your dreams? If you are . . .

> an Eskimo living in an ice hut,
> a Chinese living in a bamboo hut,
> an African living in a mud hut,
> a Bedouin living in a tent,
> an Indian living in a teepee,
> a royal living in a palace,
> a tenant living in a project,
> a slum dweller living in a shanty,
> a president living in the White House,
> a celebrity living in a penthouse,
> a peasant living in a farmhouse,
> a city dweller living in a rowhouse,

an orphan living in a foster house,
a criminal living in a prison house,
a soldier living in a guardhouse,
a beggar with no house at all . . . it doesn't matter! We all
have dreams of what home should be like.

Do you dream of a home you can never go back to, or a home
you can never have?

Do you dream of a home with love and laughter and loyalty,
with family and fun and freedom?

Do you dream of a home where you are accepted, encouraged,
and challenged, forgiven, understood, and comforted?

Do you dream of a home that never was, or a home that never
will be?

When did your home begin to unravel? Have you been blind-
sided by divorce or death or disease or depression or a thousand
and one other difficulties that have turned your dreams into a
nightmare?

There is hope! The home you've always wanted, the home you
continue to long for with all your heart, is the home God is
preparing for you! As John continued to gaze at the vision of
the glory of Jesus Christ that God revealed to him, he must
have stood in awed wonder of a "new heaven and a new earth"
(Rev. 21:1). What he saw was confirmed by the words of the
One Who was seated on the throne: "I am making everything
new!" (Rev. 21:5). Imagine it: One day, in the dream home of My
Father's House, *everything* will be brand-new!

Worth Thinking About

What can I do to make my own home more like the heaven I hope to dwell in forever? Do my children know that I love them with all my heart? Do they know I love them even when I disapprove of what they do? Are my spouse and I so committed to each other that our children experience the unity and peace of being at home in Christ?

WHEN WE ALL GET TO HEAVEN

Sing the wondrous love of Jesus,
Sing His mercy and His grace;
In the mansions bright and blessed
He'll prepare for us a place.
When we all get to heaven,
What a day of rejoicing that will be!
When we all see Jesus,
We'll sing and shout the victory.

—Eliza E. Hewitt

Prayer

DEAR FATHER, HELP ME TO WANT TO BE IN HEAVEN WITH ALL MY HEART AND TO KNOW THAT YOUR SON HAS PREPARED FOR ME A DWELLING PLACE THERE, ONE THAT I CAN TRUST WILL BE TRULY A HAPPY HOME FOR ME. MAY MY HOME NOW BE A TRUE WITNESS FOR YOU AND MAY WE LEARN HOW TO WORK OUT OUR DIFFERENCES IN A CHRIST-LIKE WAY. AMEN.

Is My Wanting to Go to Heaven Merely a Hope for "Pie in the Sky By and By"?

C. S. Lewis (1898-1963)

Skeptics mock the idea of heaven and say that those who believe in it are only engaging in wishful thinking. But if heaven is one of the hopes of a Christian, is not he or she engaging instead in hopeful thinking? C. S. Lewis, formerly a professor of Medieval and Renaissance Literature at Cambridge University and apologist for Christianity, had something to say about these matters in his book *Mere Christianity*, which was published by Macmillan in 1945 and has been in print ever since. The following excerpt is from the section of his book titled "Christian Behavior." To Lewis, heaven was a real place, as real any other place in God's creation, but with a lot of symbolic language used to convey what mere literal concepts could not convey. However, he did feel that the biblical language, though not always literal, effectively drove the church to fulfill its tasks on earth.

A continual looking forward to the eternal world is not (as some modern people think) a form of escapism or wishful thinking, but one of the things a Christian is meant to do. It does not mean that we are to leave the present world as it is. If you read history you will find that the Christians who did the most for the present world were just those who thought most of the next. The Apostles themselves, who set on foot the conversion of the Roman Empire, the great men who built up the Middle Ages, the English Evangelicals who abolished the Slave Trade, all left their mark on Earth, precisely because their minds were occupied with Heaven. It is since Christians have largely ceased to think of the other world that they have become so ineffective in this. Aim at Heaven and you will get earth "thrown in": aim at earth and you will get neither. It seems a strange rule, but something like it can be seen at work in other matters. Health is a great blessing, but the moment you make health one of your main, direct objects you start becoming a crank and imagining there is something wrong with you. You are only likely to get health provided you want other things more—food, games, work, fun, open air. In the same way, we shall never save civilisation as long as civilisation is our main object. We must learn to want something else even more.

Most of us find it very difficult to want "Heaven" at all—except in so far as "Heaven" means meeting again our friends who have died. One reason for this difficulty is that we have not been trained: our whole education tends to fix our minds on this world. Another reason is that when the real want for Heaven is present in us, we do not recognize it. Most people, if they had really learned to look into their own hearts, would know that they do want, and want acutely, something that cannot be had in this world. There are all sorts of things in this world that offer to give it to you, but they never quite keep their promise. The longings which arise in us when we first fall in love, or first think of some foreign country, or first take up some subject that excites us, are longings which no marriage, no travel, no learning, can really satisfy. I am not now speaking of what would be ordinarily called unsuccessful marriages, or holidays, or learned careers. I am speaking of the best possible ones. There was something we grasped at, in the first moment of longing, which just fades away in the reality. I think everyone knows what I mean. The wife may be a good wife, and the hotels and scenery may have been excellent, and chemistry may be a very interesting job: but some something has evaded us.

Worth Thinking About

Lewis suggests that if we aim at heaven we get "earth thrown in." What do you think he means? How can we train ourselves to want heaven so much "we get earth thrown in"? Do you know of people who are so heavenly minded they are of no great earthly good? Have you ever asked them how heaven became so real to them? Let's make it our goal to bring as much heaven to earth as we can, knowing that it is but preparation for the rest of life.

SAVIOR, AGAIN TO THY DEAR NAME

Grant us thy peace throughout our earthly life,

Our balm in sorrow and our stay in strife;

Peace to our land, the fruit of truth and love;

Peace in each heart, thy Spirit from above;

Thy peace in life, the balm of every pain;

Thy peace in death, the hope to rise again;

Then, when thy voice shall bid our conflict cease,

Call us, O Lord, to thine eternal peace.

—John Ellerton

Prayer

DEAR FATHER, HELP US TO WANT HEAVEN SO MUCH THAT WE WILL WANT TO BRING THE PRINCIPLES OF HEAVEN INTO OUR PRACTICE HERE AND NOW. HELP US TO UNDERSTAND THAT OUR DEEP LONGINGS ARE ONLY A CALL FROM YOU, AND HELP US IN OUR HEAVENLY GOALS TO MAKE EARTH A BETTER PLACE. AMEN.

How Can Reflecting on Heaven Help Me Escape the "Tyranny of the Urgent"?

St. Augustine (354–430)

InterVarsity director of faculty ministries Charles E. Hummel (1923-2004) once wrote a pamphlet called "The Tyranny of the Urgent!" There are people who can't hear this title without instantly identifying with its subject matter (which turns out to be exactly what it says it is!). They feel driven by demands on their time that they can't seem to control, the things they should have done but never got around to. For those of us who identify with the "tyranny of the urgent," we might also understand something of St. Augustine, who became Bishop of Hippo in 396 and wrote, over the next 34 years, enough material to fill fifteen volumes of a standard encyclopedia! Augustine is honored by almost all church traditions as being one of the essential 'Fathers of the church.' This hero of Christians of all denominations was obviously a busy man, yet he did not let the urgent deter him from contemplating the bliss of our Sabbath rest in the city of God. This excerpt is from his book *The City of God,* translated and published by Image Books in 1958, a division of Doubleday.

❦

Heaven, too, will be the fulfillment of that Sabbath rest foretold in the command: "Be still and see that I am God." [Ps. 46:10] This, indeed, will be that ultimate Sabbath that has no evening and which the Lord foreshadowed in the account of His creation: "And God rested on the seventh day from all his work which he had done. And he blessed the seventh day and sanctified it: because in it he had rested from all his work which God created and made." [Gen. 2:2-3] And we ourselves will be a "seventh day" when we shall be filled with His blessing and remade by His sanctification. In the stillness of that rest we shall see that He is the God whose divinity we ambitioned for ourselves when we listened to the seducer's words, "You shall be as Gods," [Gen. 3:5] and so fell away from Him, the true God who would have given us a divinity by participation that could never be gained by desertion. For, where did the doing without God end but in the undoing of man through the anger of God?

Only when we are remade by God and perfected by a greater grace shall we have the eternal stillness of that rest in which we shall see that He is God. Then only shall we be filled with Him when He will be all in all. For, although our good works are, in reality, His, they will be put to our account as payment for this Sabbath peace, so long as we do not claim them as our own; but, if we do, they will be reckoned as servile and out of place on the Sabbath, as the text reminds us: "The seventh day . . . is the rest of the Lord. . . . Thou shalt not do any work therein." [Deut. 5:14] In this connection, too, God has reminded us, through the Prophet Ezechiel: "I gave them my sabbaths, to be a sign between me and them, that they might know that I am the Lord that sanctifies them." [Eze. 20:12] It is this truth that we shall realize perfectly when we shall be perfectly at rest and shall perfectly see that it is He who is God. There is a clear indication of this final Sabbath if we take the seven ages of world history as being "days" and calculate in accordance with the data furnished by the Scriptures. The first age or day is that from Adam to the flood; the second, from the flood to Abraham. (These two "days" were not identical in length of time, but in each there were ten generations.) Then follow the three ages, each consisting of fourteen generations, as recorded in the Gospel of St. Matthew: the first, from Abraham to David; the second, from David to the transmigration to Babylon; the third, from then to Christ's nativity in the flesh. [We must keep in mind that Augustine saw genealogical continuity from generation to generation; something not necessarily done today.—Ed.] Thus, we have five ages. The sixth is the one in which we now are. It is an age not to be measured by any precise number of generations, since we are told: "It is not for you to know the times or dates which the Father has fixed by his own authority." [Acts 1:7] After this "day," God will rest on the "seventh day," in the sense that God will make us, who are to be this seventh day, rest in Him.

There is no need here to speak in detail of each of these seven "days" Suffice it to say that this "seventh day" will be our Sabbath and that it will end in no evening, but only in the Lord's day—that eighth and eternal day which dawned when Christ's resurrection heralded an eternal rest both for the spirit and for the body. On that day we shall rest and see, see and love, love and praise—for this is to be the end without the end of all our living, that Kingdom without end, and the real goal of our present life.

Worth Thinking About

While we will truly rest in heaven, what can we do now to bring rest into our lives? Consider listing some activities that you feel are dominating your life and ponder whether *all* of them are really necessary. Give yourself a break. The urgent is not always the important. Sometimes demands are placed on us by outside pressures that have nothing to do with what really needs to be done. Simplify, simplify, simplify. If you are not good at 'multitasking' do not try to make yourself do what you cannot do. Learn to be content with what you have and do not envy the one who can seem to do the impossible with nothing.

SAFELY THROUGH ANOTHER WEEK

As we come Thy name to praise, may we feel Thy presence near,

May Thy glory meet our eyes while we in Thy house appear!

Here affords us, Lord, a taste of our everlasting feast.

May Thy gospel's joyful sound conquer sinners, comfort saints;

Make the fruits of grace abound, bring relief for all complaints:

Thus may all our Sabbaths prove till we join the Church above:

Thus may all our Sabbaths prove till we join the Church above.

—John Newton

*P*rayer

DEAR FATHER, GRANT THAT SOME PART OF OUR HEAVENLY REST MIGHT BECOME REAL IN OUR DAILY LIVES AND THAT WE MIGHT ELIMINATE UNNECESSARY URGENCY THAT TROUBLES US. HELP US TO TRULY HONOR THE SABBATH AS A DAY SPECIAL TO US AND TO YOU. AMEN.

Do Those Now in Heaven Have Any Interest in Us?

Peter Kreeft

1990 saw the publication of Professor Peter Kreeft's *Everything You Ever Wanted to Know about Heaven . . . But Never Dreamed of Asking,* published by Ignatius Press. His book anticipated a good deal of liter-ature that was to come in the following years, but Dr. Kreeft's answers were uniquely his own, and they give us much to ponder. Here he reminds us that the citizens of heaven will not be so busy as to forget the activities of earth. Let us not forget that "the communion of the saints" has real value and must include those who look down from above. Do you ever think of the company of heaven and the fellow-ship that lies beyond this life?

—∞—

The living often say they feel the dead present and watching them. Is this illusion or fact?

It is a fact. The Bible says we are surrounded by "a great cloud of witnesses." [Heb. 12:1] The context is speaking of the dead. They are alive. For God is "not God of the dead, but of the living; for all live to him." [Luke 20:38]

Reason confirms revelation here. Does their love for us cease? Does it not rather increase in purity and power? And do not their vision and understanding also increase?

"The Communion of Saints" means not only (1) love and understanding among the blessed in Heaven and (2) love and understanding among the redeemed on earth but also (3) love and understanding between those two groups, the Church Militant and the Church Triumphant, temporarily separated by death.

What difference does this make? Well, what difference does it make to you if you believe you are being watched by a thousand living human eyes? Multiply this consequence by millions and by the increase in love and understanding in Heaven. Throw in literally innumerable angels, all of them sharing mightily in God's love and knowledge. Then you have the difference it makes: the exponent of infinity.

The link connecting the Church Militant with the Church Triumphant, the link connecting Heaven and earth, is the incarnate Christ. We participate in what Christ does, and Christ links Heaven and earth. He is still on earth as well as in Heaven (1) by His Spirit and (2) in His Mystical Body, the Church, His people. Christianity does not worship an absent Christ. And just as He can be on earth even when He has gone to Heaven, so can we—in Him. The cells in the one Body are all living cells, but only a very few of them are living on earth.

Worth Thinking About

For many people the thought of being looked in on or watched is anything but comforting, but we must remember that the hosts of heaven are more like a vast rooting section at a football game than they are like a peeping Tom in the skies. The heavenly company is not idly looking down on earth out of impartial disinterest. Rather, they are actively rooting for God's children to win the battle of the ages. Have you ever had the feeling that your deceased loved ones were all around you supporting you in your Christian walk? Does it give you comfort or concern to think of them with you in your work for Christ?

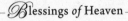

LO, WHAT A CLOUD OF WITNESSES

Lo, what a cloud of witnesses
Encompass us around;
Men once like us with suffering tried,
But now with glory crowned.
Let us, with zeal like theirs inspired,
Strive in the Christian race;
And, freed from every weight of sin,
Their holy footsteps trace.

—Anonymous

rayer

DEAR FATHER, THANK YOU THAT WE ARE NOT ALONE IN OUR STRUGGLES, BUT THERE ARE A GREAT THRONG OF PEOPLE WHO HAVE ALREADY FACED ALL THE DIFFICULTIES THAT CAN BE FACED AND NOW ROOT FOR US FROM ABOVE. HELP US TO HAVE AN UNDERSTANDING OF THE STRENGTH THAT COMES FROM THE "COMMUNION OF THE SAINTS." AMEN.

WILL WE BE SATISFIED WITH HEAVEN?

John Newton (1725–1807)

Famous author of the beloved hymn "Amazing Grace," the Reverend John Newton described himself as "once an infidel and libertine, a servant of slaves in West Africa." Later he helped lead the abolition of the slave trade in England. From 1779 until the end of his life he was Rector at St. Mary Woolnoth and friend to the mentally troubled poet William Cowper. Together they compiled and wrote hymns for a church songbook. The great misery of his early life made the promise of heaven very precious to Newton. This excerpt is from his sermon titled "The Present and Future Rest of True Believers" and is based on Matthew 11:28: "Come to Me, all you who are weary and burdened, and I will give you rest" (Matt. 11:28 NIV).

⸺◈⸺

Heaven will be a rest from unsatisfied desires. Here on earth—the more we drink, the more we thirst. But in heaven, our highest wishes shall be crowned and exceeded; we shall rest in full communion with Him whom we love; we shall no more complain of interruptions and imperfections, of an absent God, and a careless heart. Here on earth—when we obtain a little glimpse of His presence, when He brings us into His banqueting-house, and spreads His banner of love over us—how gladly would we remain in such a desirable frame! How unwilling are we to 'come down' from the mount! But these pleasing seasons are quickly ended, and often give place to some sudden unexpected trial, which robs us of all that sweetness in which we lately rejoiced.

But when we ascend the holy hill of God above, we shall never again 'come down'; we shall be forever with the Lord, never offend him, and never be separated from him again. We shall likewise rest in full conformity to him. "I will see Your face in righteousness; when I awake, I will be fully satisfied with Your presence!" (Psalm 17:15) Here on earth—we find a mixture of evil in our best moments; when we approach nearest to God, we have the liveliest sense of our defilement, and how much we fall short in every branch of duty, in every temper of our hearts. But when we shall see Jesus as he is, we shall be fully transformed into his image, and be perfectly like him!

How is this rest to be obtained? Blessed be God, in that way which alone can render it attainable by such *unworthy indigent creatures*. If it was to be *bought*—we have nothing to offer for it. If it was given as a reward of *merit*—we can do nothing to deserve it. But Jesus has said, "I will give you rest!" Our title to it cost *him* dear; he purchased it for us with his own blood; but to us it comes freely. Sincere faith in Jesus puts us in immediate possession of the first-fruits, the pledge of this inheritance; and faith will lead us powerfully and safely, through all hindrances and enemies, to the full enjoyment of the whole.

Faith unites us to Christ; gives us an immediate interest in all the benefits of his life, death, and intercession; opens the way of communication for all needful supplies of grace here, and insures to us the accomplishment of all the Lord has spoken to us of, in a state of glory. "He who *believes* shall be saved;" (Mark 16:16) —saved in defiance of all the opposition of earth and hell; saved, notwithstanding he is in himself *unstable* as water, *weak* as a bruised reed, and *helpless* as a newborn babe! What Jesus will give—none can take away. Only remember that it is a *free gift*. Receive it thankfully—and rejoice in the Giver. Let him have all the glory of his own undertaking. Renounce every other *hope* and every other *plea*—but his promise and mediation. Commit your souls to him—and then fear nothing. "The eternal God is your refuge, and underneath are the everlasting arms!" (Deu. 33:27) He will *fight* your battles, *heal* your wounds, *refresh* your fainting spirits, *guide* you by his counsel while here, and at last *receive* you to himself!

May we not therefore say, 'Happy are the people who are in such a case! Happy they, who have been enabled to accept this gracious invitation, who have already entered upon the rest of grace, and have a well-grounded expectation that they shall rest in glory!'

Believers, what should you fear, or why complain? Look *back* to where the Lord found you dead in sin, helpless and hopeless, and insensible of your danger! Look *forward* to what he has provided for you—a crown of life, and a kingdom that cannot be shaken. "For God has reserved a priceless inheritance for his children. It is kept in heaven for you, pure and undefiled, beyond the reach of change and decay!" (1 Peter 1:4) Think of the love, the sufferings, the glory of *him* to whom you owe these blessings—and let these considerations animate you to run with patience (Hebrews 12:1) and thankfulness, the race that is set before you.

Worth Thinking About

Newton used the word *wretch* in the hymn *Amazing Grace* to describe his state of being outside of Christ. How would Newton describe the state of the person who seeks Christ's rest? If there is an opposite to the word *wretch*, no single world will do, but the repentant *wretched* do become the *blessed* of heaven. "Come to me, all you who labor

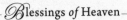

and are heavy laden, and I will give you rest" (Matt. 11:28). Can you testify that his "yoke is easy" and his "burden is light" when you rest in him?

AMAZING GRACE

Amazing grace, how sweet the sound that saved a wretch like me!

I once was lost but now am found, was blind, but now I see.

'Twas grace that taught my heart to fear, and grace my fear relieved;

How precious did that grace appear the hour I first believed!

—John Newton

When we've been there ten thousand years, bright shining as the sun,

We've no less days to sing God's praise than when we'd first begun.

—Anonymous

rayer

DEAR FATHER, HELP US TO PARTAKE OF YOUR PROVISION OF HEAVEN AND LEARN TO BE SATISFIED WITH THE PORTION WE RECEIVE NOW ON EARTH. HELP US TO LOOK FORWARD TO THE CROWN OF LIFE WHICH WILL MAKE ALL OUR LABORS WORTH IT ALL. AMEN.

Will I Be the Same Person in Heaven That I Now Am on Earth?

Because Jesus was resurrected in a transformed body that looked different from the one he had from his Incarnation, some Christians have wondered about whether their personalities will be changed in heaven just as their bodies are changed. After all, going from being an earthly sinner to a totally sanctified person must make some changes in our personalities! What would a sinless me be like? What is the significance of having a new body in the resurrection? Since founding Eternal Perspectives Ministry in 1990, former pastor Randy Alcorn has published over forty books on topics related to eternity and heaven. His books have sold some seven million copies. This excerpt is from Alcorn's book _Heaven_, published by Tyndale House in 2004 and provides some useful insights into these questions.

In Dickens' _A Christmas Carol_, Ebenezer Scrooge was terrified when he saw a phantom.

"What are you?" Scrooge asked.

"Ask me who I was," the ghost replied.

"Who were you then?" said Scrooge. . . .

"In life I was your partner, Jacob Marley."

Disembodied spirits aren't who they once were. Continuity of identity ultimately requires bodily resurrection.

In the Movie _2010_, David Bowman appears in ghostly form. When asked who he is, he replies, "I _was_ David Bowman."

Unless we grasp the resurrection, we won't believe that we'll continue to be ourselves in the afterlife. We are physical beings. If the eternal Heaven is a disembodied state, then our humanity will either be diminished or transcended, and we will never again be ourselves after we die.

Contrast Jacob Marley and David Bowman with Job and Jesus. Job said, "In my flesh I will see God; . . . I, and not another" (Job 19:26-27). The risen Christ said, "Look at my hands and my feet. It is I myself! Touch me and see; a ghost does not have flesh and bones, as you see I have" (Luke 24:39).

Jesus called people in Heaven by name, including Lazarus in the intermediate Heaven (Luke 16:25) and Abraham, Isaac, and Jacob in the eternal Heaven (Matthew 8:11). A name denotes a distinct identity, an individual. The fact that people in Heaven can be called by the same name they had on Earth demonstrates they remain the same people. In Heaven I'll be Randy Alcorn—without the bad parts—forever. If you know Jesus, you'll be you—without the bad parts—forever.

WILL WE BE UNIQUE?

Just as our genetic code and fingerprints are unique now, we should expect the same of our new bodies. Individual identity is an essential aspect of personhood. God is the creator of individual identities and personalities. He makes no two snowflakes, much less two people, alike. Not even "identical twins" are identical. Individuality preceded sin and the Curse. Individuality was God's plan from the beginning.

Heaven's inhabitants don't simply rejoice over nameless multitudes coming to God. They rejoice over each and every person (Luke 15:4-7, 10). That's a powerful affirmation of Heaven's view of each person as a separate individual whose life is observed and cared for one at a time. . . .

In his book *The Problem of Pain*, C. S. Lewis expressed his awe at the diversity with which God created us: "If He had no use for all these differences, I do not see why He should have created more souls than one. . . . Your soul has a curious shape because it is a hollow made to fit a particular swelling in the infinite contours of the divine substance, or a key to unlock one of the doors in the house with many mansions. For it is not humanity in the abstract that is to be saved, but you—you, the individual reader, John Stubbs or Janet Smith. . . . Your place in heaven will seem to be made for you and you alone, because you were made for it—made for it stitch as a glove is made for a hand."

Worth Thinking About

No two snowflakes are alike and no two people are alike. Have you ever tried to imagine what your heavenly personality will be like? You won't just be busy avoiding sin, you will actually be in complete fellowship with the Father, always doing what is pleasing in his sight because you *want* to do it. The practical consequences of this change in our hearts must be amazing. Decisions, if they can be called that, will be made without the hindrance of sin pushing us in the wrong direction. We will be ourselves, yet the common temptations that have always defeated us before will be unknown, perhaps not even remembered. Whatever doing the will of God is in heaven, we will be doing it personally because we truly enjoy pleasing the Father, and the joy will completely satisfy us.

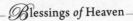

LET ALL THE WORLD IN EVERY CORNER SING

Let all the world in every corner sing: My God and King!
The heavens are not too high His praise may thither fly;
The earth is not too low His praises there may grow.
Let all the world in every corner sing: My God and King!

—George Herbert

rayer

DEAR FATHER, HELP US TO WANT TO FREELY DO YOUR WILL NOW SO THAT WE MAY BE INCREASINGLY FITTED FOR HEAVEN AND IN PRACTICE FOR THE JOYS TO COME. THANK YOU THAT WE WILL STILL BE THE UNIQUE PEOPLE YOU HAVE MADE US TO BE AND THAT WE WILL BE MORE OURSELVES AND YET MORE YOURS THAN WE'VE EVER BEEN. AMEN.

Does My Heavenly Home Have a Location?

D. L. Moody

One of our most basic questions is about the location of heaven. The theories are many and no one can have all the answers, but as American evangelist D.L. Moody pointed out, for most of us, the biblical picture is a good one by which to address the question. But first we have to ask, by "heaven's location," do we mean a spot in the universe, like a planet that anyone might find by a telescope or do we mean merely its position in location to us as inhabitants of the earthly globe? Moody's practical answer is simply that heaven is "up" as hell is "down" from any position we may inhabit on earth. This biblically referenced answer is satisfactory, not because it actually locates heaven somewhere in the physical universe, but because it locates heaven positionally, with reference to where we ourselves are. And that is all we need to know—until we know more someday. This excerpt is from his book *Heaven: Where It Is, Its Inhabitants, and How to Get There.*

—❧—

I do not think that it is wrong for us to think and talk about heaven. I like to locate heaven, and find out all I can about it. I expect to live there through all eternity. If I was going to dwell in any place in this country, if I was going to make it my home, I would want to inquire about the place, about its climate, about the neighbors I would have, and about everything, in fact, that I could learn concerning it. If any of you were going to emigrate, that would be the way you would feel. Well, we are all going to emigrate in a very little while to a country that is very far away. We are going to spend eternity in another world, a grand and glorious world where God reigns. Is it not natural, then, that we should look and listen and try to find out who is already there, and what is the route to take? Soon after I was converted, an infidel asked me one day why I looked up when I prayed. He said that heaven was no more above as than below us; that heaven was everywhere. Well, I was greatly bewildered, and the next time I prayed, it seemed almost as if I was praying into the air. Since then I have become better acquainted with the Bible, and I have come to see that heaven is above us; that it is upward and not downward. The spirit of God is everywhere, but God is in heaven, and heaven is above our heads. It does not matter what part of the globe we may stand upon, heaven is above us.

In the 17th chapter of Genesis it says that God went up from Abraham; and in the third chapter of John, that he came down from heaven. So, in the 1st chapter of Acts we find that Christ went up into heaven (not down), and a cloud received him out of sight: thus we see heaven is up. The very arrangement of the firmament about the earth declares the seat of God's glory to be above us. Job says, "Let not God regard it from above," [Job 3:4] and we find the Psalmist declaring, "the Lord is high above nations, and His glory above the heavens." [Ps. 113:4]

Again in Deuteronomy, we find, "who shall go up for us to heaven?" [Deut. 30:12] Thus, all through scripture we find that we are given the location of heaven as upward and beyond the firmament. This firmament, with its many bright worlds scattered through, is so vast that heaven must be an extensive realm. Yet this need not surprise us.

It is not for short-sighted man to inquire why God made heaven so extensive that its lights along the way can be seen from any part or side of this little world.

In the 51st chapter of the prophecy of Jeremiah we are told that: "He hath made the earth by his power; he hath established the world by his wisdom, and hath stretched out the heaven by his understanding." Yet, how little we really know of that power, or wisdom or understanding! As it says in the 26th chapter of Job: "Lo, these are parts of his ways: but how little a portion is heard of him? But the thunder of his power, who can understand?"

This is the word of God. As we find in the 42nd chapter of Isaiah: "Thus saith God the Lord, he that created the heavens and stretched them out; he that spread forth the earth, and that which cometh out of it; he that giveth bread unto the people upon it, and spirit to them that walk within." The discernment of God's power, the messages of heaven, do not always come in great things. We read in the 19th chapter of the first book of Kings:

> "And behold, the Lord passed by, and a great and strong wind rent the mountains, and brake in pieces the rocks before the Lord; but the Lord was not in the wind: and after the wind an earthquake; but the Lord was not in the earthquake: and after the earthquake a fire; but the Lord was not in the fire: and after the fire a still small voice."

It is as a still small voice that God speaks to His children. [1 Kings 19:11-13]

Some people are trying to find out just how far heaven is away. There is one thing we know about it; that is, that it is not so far away but that God can hear us when we pray. I do not believe there has ever been a tear shed for sin since Adam's fall in Eden to the present time, but God has witnessed that. He is not too far from this earth for us to go to Him; and if there is a sigh that comes from a burdened heart to-day, God will hear that sigh. If there is a cry coming up from a heart broken on account of sin, God will hear that cry; He is not so far away, heaven is not so far away, as to be inaccessible to the smallest child. In the 7th chapter and 14th verse of Second Chronicles, we read:

> "If my people, which are called by my name, shall humble themselves, and pray, and seek my face, and turn from their wicked ways, then will I hear from heaven, and will forgive their sins, and will heal their land,"

When I was in Dublin, they were telling me about a father who had lost a little boy, and he had not thought about the future, he had been so entirely taken up with this world and its affairs; but when that little boy his only child, died, that father's heart was broken, and every night when he got home from work, they would find him with his tallow candle and his Bible in his room, and he was hunting up all that he could find there about heaven. And someone asked him what he was doing, and he said he was trying to find out where his child had gone, and I think he was a reasonable man. I suppose there is not a man or woman but has dear ones that are gone. Shall we close this book to-day? Or shall we look into it to try to find where the loved ones are?

I was reading, some time ago, an account of a father, a minister, who had lost a child. He had gone to a great many funerals, offering comfort to others in sorrow, but now the iron had entered his own soul, and a brother minister had come to officiate and preach the funeral sermon; and after the minister got through speaking, the father got up, and standing right at the head of the coffin, looking at the face of that loved child that was gone, he said that a few years ago, when he had first come into that parish, as he used to look over the river he took no interest in the people over there, because they were all strangers to him and there were none over there that belonged to his parish. But, he said a few years ago a young man came into his home, and married his daughter, and she went over the river to live, and when that child went over there, he became suddenly interested in the inhabitants, and every morning as he would get up he would look out of the window and look over there at her home. But now, said he, another child has been taken. She has gone over another river, and heaven seems dearer and nearer to me than it ever has before.

My friends, let us believe this good old Book, that heaven is not a myth, and let us be prepared to follow the dear ones who have gone before. There, and there alone, can we find the peace we seek for.

Worth Thinking About

Whatever spurs your heart to think of heavenly things must be good; because when you think about it, you want to prepare yourself to go there and be forever in fellowship with Jesus and others you love. What are the scriptural references to heaven that most intrigue you, most stir your imagination, and most capture your heart?

WHEN WE ALL GET TO HEAVEN

Sing the wondrous love of Jesus,

Sing His mercy and his grace.

In the mansions bright and blessed

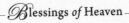

He'll prepare for us a place. . . .
Let us then be true and faithful,
Trusting, serving every day;
Just one glimpse of Him in glory
Will the toils of life repay.
—Eliza E. Hewitt

Prayer

DEAR FATHER, I WANT TO BE WITH YOU AND MY LOVED ONES IN HEAVEN. HELP ME PUT AWAY THE TEMPTATIONS OF SIN AND FOLLOW YOU AND YOUR HOLY WILL, KNOWING YOUR GRACE IS SUFFICIENT FOR MY EVERY NEED. GRANT THAT I WILL UNDERSTAND YOUR WORDS ABOUT HEAVEN GIVEN IN YOUR HOLY WORD. AMEN.

What Will It Be Like to Have a Perfect Body?

Joni Eareckson Tada

Followers of Christ appear divided over how they receive the news that they will get a new body as a result of the resurrection and the new life they will have in heaven. Some are excited that they will finally be able to lose those "extra" pounds or rise from their wheel chairs; others think very little of their body at all and almost prefer the Greek notion of being a disembodied spirit. Joni Eareckson Tada suffered a spinal injury in a diving accident when she was just seventeen. Over the years she has come to have an international speaking ministry, and *Joni and Friends*, an organization that she founded, advocates for the handicapped. *Heaven: Your Real Home*, published by Zondervan in 1995, addresses the significance of the new body she will have in her future life. In this passage, Joni explores what the joys of a new body will bring.

I still can hardly believe it. I, with shriveled, bent fingers, atrophied muscles, gnarled knees, and no feeling from the shoulders down, will one day have a new body, light, bright, and clothed in righteousness—powerful and dazzling.

Can you imagine the hope this gives someone spinal cord-injured like me? Or someone who is cerebral palsied, brain-injured, or who has multiple sclerosis? Imagine the hope this gives someone who is manic depressive. No other religion, no other philosophy promises new bodies, hearts, and minds. Only in the Gospel of Christ do hurting people find such incredible hope.

It's easy for me to "be joyful in hope," as it says in Romans 12:12, and that's exactly what I've been doing for the past twenty-odd years. My assurance of heaven is so alive that I've been making dates with friends to do all sorts of fun things once we get our new bodies—like the following conversation with a girl in a wheelchair I met at a conference.

"Since we've been sitting here talking about heaven," I said, "would you like to make a date to get together up there?"

The girl, sitting twisted and humped over, gave me a funny look and asked, "And do what?"

"What would you like to do?"

Uh . . . I'd like to be able to knit," she said hesitantly.

"Then let's make a date to meet in a cabin, pull up a couple rocking chairs by the fireplace, and reach for our knitting needles, okay?"

My friend in the wheelchair scoffed, "You're just saying that. Heaven's not going to have cabins and rocking chairs. That stuff's only on earth."

I looked at her in all seriousness and said, "I believe heaven will. Heaven is by no means ambiguous; Isaiah 65:17 says that God is planning 'new heavens and a new earth.' Did you get that? Heaven has our planet in it. A new earth with earthy things in it. Nothing clunky . . . no gawky images . . . just warm and wonderful things that make earth . . . *earth*."

"How can you be so sure of what the new earth will be like?"

"'Cause I don't think God is going to switch dictionaries on us and suddenly redefine what *earth* is. If there are streets, rivers, trees, and mountains in the new earth, like the Bible says there will be, then why not all the other good things? Why not . . . rocking chairs?"

She sat looking at me with a wry smile and then her skepticism vanished. She started deliberating on which sweater pattern to use. She learned what most people discover after spending a few minutes talking to me. I take heaven seriously.

I take it as seriously as do children. One morning while I was waiting in an airport, I told my five-year-old friend, Matthew Fenlason, and his little brother, Stephen, to grab hold of the arm of my wheelchair and come with me to look for some kids with whom we could play. We found a couple of little boys sitting with their parents in the waiting area, and I asked if they would like to play a game with us. Within minutes, in the open area of the airport lounge, we started a game of Duck-Duck-Goose. When Matthew tagged me "goose," I raced in my wheelchair around the circle of children, but I couldn't catch him. Feeling badly that I wasn't able to get up and run, he whispered, "Don't worry, Joni, when we get to heaven your legs will work, and we'll be able to *really* play Duck-Duck-Goose."

He meant it. And so did I.

Rana Leavell and I plan to climb the mountains behind the Rose Bowl. Thad Mandsager and I, both quads, will ski the Sierras. My sisters Linda, Kathy, Jay, and I are going to play doubles tennis. Michael Lynch plans to teach me how to dance the *paso doble*, and my husband, Ken, has already said, "I don't mind who fills up your dance card in heaven . . . but save the last one for me." I have a whole circle of Romanian orphans I want to take picnicking on the Hungarian plains, and I can't wait to put my friend Judy Butler on a really fast horse and go racing across Windsor Great Park.

Horses in heaven? Yes, I think animals are some of God's best and most avant-garde ideas; why would He throw out His greatest creative achievements? I'm not talking about my pet schnauzer, Scrappy, dying and going to heaven—Ecclesiastes 3:21 puts the brakes on that idea ["Who knows if the spirit of man rises upward and if the spirit of the animal goes down into the earth?" NIV—Ed.]. I'm talking about new animals fit for a new order of things. Isaiah foresaw lions and lambs lying down together, as well as bears, cows, and cobras; and John foresaw the saints galloping on white horses. I have no idea where they will fit, but I'm certain they will populate part of the new heavens and new earth. Again, underline that word "earth." It just wouldn't be "earth" without animals. So, if you want to go horseback riding, meet Judy and me at the statue of the Copper Horse at the end of the bridle path in Windsor.

You can tell I don't take these appointments lightly. I'm convinced these things will really happen. Goodness, I thought my friend under the white cabana next to the swimming pool was pleased to see me in a glorified state, just think of the pleasure we all will experience to see each other sin-free with glowing bodies all light and bright. It will be the answer to all our longings.

And not only our longings, but those of Jesus.

Worth Thinking About

Jesus accepted his earthly body, apparently without embarrassment: he did not regard it as an object either to be mistreated or indulged. What can the Lord do with his new body that he couldn't do with his old one (which was not sinful, for he had nothing to do with sin)? We know little except that he had access to his disciples whenever he chose, could eat food, show his scars, and pass through walls. Could it be that always having had bodies we would be somehow spiritually incomplete without one? Whatever our new bodies will be like it is going to be exciting to discover what we can do with them!

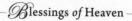

OUR NEW BODIES

So also is the resurrection of the dead. The body is sown in corruption, it is raised in incorruption. It is sown in dishonor, it is raised in glory. It is sown in weakness, it is raised in power. It is sown a natural body, it is raised a spiritual body. There is a natural body, and there is a spiritual body. And so it is written, *"The first man Adam became a living being."* The last Adam became a life-giving spirit.—1 Corinthians 15:42-45

Prayer

DEAR FATHER, WE THANK YOU THAT HAVING OUR OLD BODY DOES NOT MAKE US UNACCEPTABLE TO YOU. YET WE ARE THANKFUL ALSO THAT YOU WANT US TO HAVE A NEW BODY THAT WILL LEAVE BEHIND THE OLD IMPERFECTIONS OF DISEASE, DECAY, AND INJURY. THANK YOU THAT WE WILL ONE DAY BE GETTING NEW BODIES WITH AMAZING ABILITIES BEYOND OUR WILDEST DREAMS. AMEN.

How Can Thoughts of Heaven Comfort Me in My Trials and Help Me Achieve Peace of Heart?

C. H. Spurgeon (1834–1892)

Although it is by no means a universal Christian experience, some believers have learned so to dwell on their heavenly blessings that they are enabled to remain calm through the turmoil of everyday life. The Rev. Charles Haddon Spurgeon was perhaps the most famous Baptist preacher of his day. Converted at the age of sixteen, he began his ministry as a preacher almost immediately. Eventually, he became the founding pastor of The Metropolitan Tabernacle of London where his congregation grew to a membership of 5,000 souls. Spurgeon delivered the whole of this sermon at New Park Street Church, Southwark, England in 1855 at the tender age of twenty-one. May the kind of maturity and peace of mind demonstrated by this message help us to "so shine before men," that they may see our good works and glorify our Father in heaven (Matt. 5:16).

As it is written, eye hath not seen, nor ear heard, neither have entered into the heart of man, the things which God hath prepared for them that love him. But God hath revealed *them* unto us by his Spirit; for the Spirit searcheth all things, yea, the deep things of God.—1 Corinthians 2:9–10. . . .

We think a Christian gets a gaze of what heaven is *when in the midst of trials and troubles he is able to cast all his care upon the Lord* because he cares for him. When waves of distress, and billows of affliction pass over the Christian, there are times when his faith is so strong that he lies down and sleeps, though the hurricane is thundering in his ears, and though billows are rocking him like a child in its cradle, though the earth is removed, and the mountains are carried into the midst of the sea, he says, "God is our refuge and strength, a very present help in trouble." [Ps. 46:1] Famine and desolation come; but he says, "Though the fig tree shall not blossom, neither shall there be fruit on the vine, though the labour of the olive shall fail, and the field shall yield no increase, yet will I trust in the Lord, and stay myself on the God of Jacob." [Hab. 3:17] Affliction smites him to the ground; he looks up, and says, "Though he slay me, yet will I trust in him." [Job 13:15] The blows that are given to him are like the lashing of a whip upon the water, covered up immediately, and he seems to feel nothing. It is not stoicism; it is the peculiar sleep of the beloved. "So he giveth his beloved sleep." [Ps. 127:2] Persecution surrounds him; but he is unmoved. Heaven is something like that — a place of holy calm and trust—

> That holy calm, that sweet repose,
> Which none but he who feels it knows.
> This heavenly calm within the breast
> Is the dear pledge of glorious rest,
> Which for the church of God remains,
> The end of cares, the end of pains.

But there is another season in which the Christian has heaven revealed to him; and that is, *the season of quiet contemplation.* There are precious hours, blessed be God, when we forget the world—times and seasons when we get quite away from it, when our weary spirit wings its way far, far, from scenes of toil and strife. There are precious moments when the angel of contemplation gives us a vision. He comes and puts his finger on the lip of the noisy world; he bids the wheels that are continually rattling in our ears be still; and we sit down, and there is a solemn silence of the mind. We find our heaven and our God; we engage ourselves in contemplating the glories of Jesus, or mounting upwards towards the bliss of heaven—in going backward to the great secrets of electing love, in considering the immutability of the blessed covenant, in thinking of that wind which "bloweth where it listeth," [John 3:8] in remembering our own participation of that life which comes from God, in thinking of our blood-bought union with the Lamb, of the consummation of our marriage with him in realms of light and bliss, or any such kindred topics. Then it is that we know a little about heaven. Have you never found, you sons and daughters of gaiety, a holy calm come over you at times, in reading the thoughts of your fellowmen? But how blessed to come and read the thoughts of God, and work, and weave them out in contemplation. Then we have a web of contemplation that we wrap around us like an enchanted garment, and we open our eyes and see heaven. Christian! when you are enabled by the Spirit to hold a season of sweet contemplation, then you can say—"But he hath revealed them unto us by his Spirit;" [1 Cor. 2:10] for the joys of heaven are akin to the joys of contemplation, and the joys of a holy calm in God. But there are times with me—I dare say there may be with some of you—when we do something more than contemplate—when we arise by meditation above thought itself, and when our soul, after having touched the Pisgah of contemplation by the way, flies positively into the heavenly places in Christ Jesus. There are seasons when the Spirit not only stands and flaps his wings over the gulf, but positively crosses the Jordan and dwells with Christ, holds fellowship with angels, and talks with spirits—gets up there with Jesus, clasps him in his arms, and cries, "My beloved is mine, and I am his; I will hold him, and will not let him go." [Song 2:16] I know what it is at times to lay my beating head on the bosom of Christ with something more than faith—actually and positively to get hold of him; not only to take him by faith, but actually and positively to feed on him; to feel a vital union with him, to grasp his arm, and feel his very pulse beating. You say. "Tell it not to unbelievers; they will laugh!" Laugh you may; but when we are there we care not for your laughter, if you should laugh as loud as devils; for one moment's fellowship with Jesus would recompense us for it all. Picture not fairy lands; this is heaven, this is bliss. "He hath revealed it unto us by his Spirit." [1 Cor. 2:10]

Worth Thinking About

How can we make time in our schedule, however busy, to leave times for "contemplation" or meditation that our souls might fly "positively into the heavenly places in Christ Jesus"? Could you devote just 15 minutes a day to reading Scripture and saying prayers? Many truly busy people find they can learn to do devotions on the run with their Bibles and prayer books open on their desks. Sometimes the prayer closet just isn't handy!

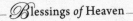
JESUS, LOVER OF MY SOUL

Jesus, Lover of my soul, let me to Thy bosom fly,

While the nearer waters roll, while the tempest still is high!

Hide me, O my Savior hide, till the storm of life is past;

Safe into the haven guide, O receive my soul at last!

—Charles Wesley

Prayer

DEAR FATHER, GRANT US THE WILL AND THE OPPORTUNITY TO MAKE TIME FOR YOU EACH DAY. HELP US TO COUNT OUR BLESSINGS AND NOURISH OURSELVES ON YOUR PROMISES OF PROVISION FOR YOUR CHILDREN. MAY WE LEARN TO CONTEMPLATE ALL THAT HEAVEN HAS IN STORE. AMEN.

How Can I Be Sure I Will Go to Heaven?

Tim LaHaye

One of the most popular Christian authors over the last thirty years has been Tim LaHaye who, along with Jerry Jenkins, teamed up to write the successful *Left Behind* series of novels about end-times prophecy. Dr. LaHaye was the long-time pastor of Scott Memorial Baptist Church in San Diego where he also founded Christian Heritage College and the Institute for Creation Research along with other founders. Here Dr. LaHaye, the author of some forty books, writes about how not to be left behind. His explanation of the Gospel emphasizes the importance of truly hearing the word of God and of believing in Jesus Christ for salvation. This selection comes from his bestseller *The Merciful God of Prophecy: His Loving Plan for You in the End Times,* published by Warner Books in 2002.

∞

God Wants Us to Live Forever with Him

We all aspire to a long life, and the older we get, the more we want to add years to the calendar. But all of us know one thing about life; it ends, sooner or later. And what *then?*

We're all born with the knowledge that we are not meant only for this world. We intuitively believe we will live again. Almost every religion in the world has some idea, no matter how vague, of life after death. Where did they all get such an idea? Collusion? A desperate desire to deny human mortality? No. Ecclesiastes 3:11 tells us that God has "set eternity in the hearts of men" (NIV).

God loves us, and wants us to spend eternity with him in heaven. That's why Jesus came to earth, to make it possible for his Father's desire to be fulfilled. "Whoever lives and believes in Me shall never die," he said in John 11:26. Oh, one's body will die, but the real person who indwells that body will live forever.

In heaven at this very moment, Joseph of Arimathea could be having a spirited conversation with Joseph, the former prince of Egypt. Martin Luther could be discussing theology with Augustine of Hippo. And Mary Magdalene might be sipping celestial tea around a table of friends, perhaps with the former judge Deborah, the former nun Teresa of Avila, and the former nurse Florence Nightingale. They're all enjoying eternal life in the presence of God.

Jesus did all he could to broadcast the wonderful message of life in him. In one of my favorite passages, he told a crowd, "Most assuredly, I say to you, he who hears My word and believes in Him who sent Me has everlasting life, and shall not come into judgment, but has passed from death into life" (John 5:24).

What are the keys? The Bible gives us two: *hearing* the word of Jesus and *believing* it. The word "believe" in the passage we just read could be translated "commit." Whoever believes enough in Jesus to commit his or her life to him has everlasting life. What person with any sense would refuse the offer of eternal life?

When we know we have received life everlasting, we no longer have to fear death. As a pastor for many years, I've stood at the bedside of many individuals who were either dying or on the verge of death. While Christians aren't anxious to die, they're not afraid, either. In fact, many believers get a premonition when it comes time to go home.

Just recently I heard about a seriously ill believer who told his friends that he really wanted to live. But one day he changed his tune. He calmly announced, "The Lord told me I'm going to die." Six days later, he slipped away, without any fear and with absolute peace.

How could a sinful human being ever die so serenely? How could a flawed mortal slip into eternity without the slightest bit of apprehension? Believers in Jesus can do so, because "the testimony of Jesus is the Spirit of prophecy," and he wants to give us the assurance of eternal life.

Now, can you love a God like that?

Worth Thinking About

Dr. LaHaye points out that the requirements for becoming a child of God are simple: hear the message of Jesus and believe he is your savior from sin. Of course, by hearing and believing in Jesus, Dr. LaHaye means that we actually take Jesus message to heart and follow him by doing what he says. In doing this, we are actually storing up for ourselves treasures in heaven. What does it take for you to hear and believe the message?

I AM TRUSTING THEE, LORD JESUS

I am trusting Thee, Lord Jesus, trusting only Thee;
Trusting Thee for full salvation, great and free.
I am trusting Thee for pardon; at Thy feet I bow,
For Thy grace and tender mercy, trusting now.

—Francis Ridley Havergal

Prayer

DEAR FATHER, THANK YOU THAT YOUR SALVATION COMES AS A GIFT THROUGH YOUR SON, JESUS CHRIST. HELP US TO TRUST AND BELIEVE IN YOU SO THAT WE TOO MAY HAVE EVERLASTING LIFE. AMEN.

What Am I to Make of Some Special Revelation of the Lord That Is Precious to Me But Is Not Manifested in Scripture?

Matthew Henry (1662-1714)

Matthew Henry's Commentary on the Whole Bible is still regarded as a classic and is recommended by such theologians as R. C. Sproul. Henry was a Presbyterian minister whose *Commentary* had to be completed by others and wasn't published until 1811. Although his work is over two hundred years old and is pastoral in nature, its devotional insight remains cherished. Henry values our personal experiences with God but cautions us to make much more of scriptural revelation than of any private experience. Any personal visitations must be treated with humility and not used as an excuse for spiritual pride or to ignore the plain teaching of Scripture.

It is not expedient for me doubtless to glory. I will come to visions and revelations of the Lord. I knew a man in Christ above fourteen years ago, (whether in the body, I cannot tell; or whether out of the body, I cannot tell: God knoweth) such an one caught up to the third heaven. And I knew such a man (whether in the body, or out of the body, I cannot tell: God knoweth), how that he was caught up into paradise, and heard unspeakable words, which it is not lawful for a man to utter. Of such an one will I glory: yet of myself I will not glory, but in mine infirmities. For though I would desire to glory, I shall not be a fool; for I will say the truth: but now I forbear, lest any man should think of me above that which he seeth me to be, or that he heareth of me.—2 Cor. 12:1-6

Here we may observe the narrative the apostle gives of the favours God had shown him, and the honour he had done him; for doubtless he himself is the man in Christ of whom he speaks. Concerning this we may take notice, 1. Of the honour itself which was done to the apostle: he was *caught up into the third heaven,* v. 2. When this was we cannot say, whether it was during those three days that he lay without sight at his conversion or at some other time afterwards, much less can we pretend to say *how* this was, whether by a separation of his soul from his body or by an extraordinary transport in the depth of contemplation. It would be presumption for us to determine, if not also to enquire into, this matter, seeing the apostle himself says, *Whether in the body or out of the body, I cannot tell.* It was certainly a very extraordinary honour done him: in some sense he was caught up into the *third heaven,* the heaven of the blessed, above the aërial heaven, in which the fowls fly, above the starry heaven, which is adorned with those glorious orbs: it was into the third heaven, where God most eminently manifests his glory.

We are not capable of knowing all, nor is it fit we should know very much . . . ; it is our duty and interest to give diligence to make sure to ourselves a mansion [*room*—Ed.] there; and, if that be cleared up to us, then we should long to be removed thither, to abide there for ever. This third heaven is called paradise (v. 4), in allusion to the earthly paradise out of which Adam was driven for his transgression; it is called the paradise of God

(Rev. ii. 7), signifying to us that by Christ we are restored to all the joys and honours we lost by sin, yea, to much better.

The apostle does not mention what he saw in the third heaven or paradise, but tells us that *he heard unspeakable words*, such as it is not possible for a man to utter—such are the sublimity of the matter and our unacquaintedness with the language of the upper world: nor was it lawful to utter those words, because, while we are here in this world, we have a more sure word of prophecy than such visions and revelations. 2 Pet. i. 19. We read of the tongue of angels as well as men, and Paul knew as much of that as ever any man upon earth did, and yet preferred charity, that is, the sincere love of God and our neighbour. This account which the apostle gives us of his vision should check our curious desires after forbidden knowledge, and teach us to improve the revelation God has given us in his word. Paul himself, who had been in the third heaven, did not publish to the world what he had heard there, but adhered to the doctrine of Christ: on this foundation the church is built, and on this we must build our faith and hope.

The modest and humble manner in which the apostle mentions this matter is observable. One would be apt to think that one who had had such visions and revelations as these would have boasted greatly of them; but, says he, *It is not expedient for me doubtless to glory*, v. 1. He therefore did not mention this immediately, nor till *above fourteen years* after, v. 2. And then it is not without some reluctancy, as a thing which in a manner he was forced to by the necessity of the case. Again, he speaks of himself in the third person, and does not say, I am the man who was thus honoured above other men. Again, his humility appears by the check he seems to put upon himself (v. 6), which plainly shows that he delighted not to dwell upon this theme. Thus was he, who was not behind the chief of the apostles in dignity, very eminent for his humility. Note, it is an excellent thing to have a lowly spirit in the midst of high advancements; and those who abase themselves shall be exalted.

Worth Thinking About

It is not unusual for Christians to talk about what they think God has been teaching them or showing them either through Scripture or personal experience. Sometimes we make much of an answered prayer that has impressed or even startled us, because we didn't think God could or would do what we asked. How can we learn to keep ourselves humble after a "mountain top" experience? How can we hold fast to God Himself?

BENEATH THE CROSS OF JESUS

Beneath the cross of Jesus I fain would take my stand,

The shadow of a mighty rock within a weary land;

A home within the wilderness, a rest upon the way,

From the burning of the noontide heat, and the burden of the day. . . .

I take, O cross, thy shadow for my abiding place;

I ask no other sunshine than the sunshine of His face;

Content to let the world go by, to know no gain or loss,

My sinful self my only shame, my glory all the cross.

—Elizabeth C. Clephane

Prayer

DEAR FATHER, GUARD OUR HEARTS FROM SPIRITUAL PRIDE THAT MAKES MUCH OF WHAT WE HAVE EXPERIENCED BUT WHICH SOMETIMES TEMPTS US TO FORGET WHAT YOU HAVE DONE FOR US WITHOUT OUR DESERVING OR EVEN ASKING FOR YOUR HELP. GUIDE US TO READ SCRIPTURE AS THE REAL SOURCE OF OUR UNDERSTANDING OF YOU AND YOUR WILL. AMEN.

Will Children Enjoy Heaven?

G. Campbell Morgan (1863-1945)

In the view of this English pastor, heaven will be a fit place for children, and that in itself tells us much about the glory of the New Jerusalem where heaven reigns supreme. Children will be at play there, G. Campbell Morgan believes. Dr. Morgan once said that his father was such a good example of the faith it would have been impossible for him not to have become a Christian, and Morgan dedicated his life to Christian service. Morgan served as an ordained Congregationalist minister at Westminster Church in London and also traveled throughout the United States. His habit of smoking cigars alarmed some of his American friends, but those so alarmed learned to tolerate his habit for the sake of hearing his sermons. Morgan's thoughts on the City of God from Zechariah come from his sermon "The Children's Playground in the City of God" found in the volume *The Westminster Pulpit,* published by Hodder and Stoughton in 1916. It should be noted here that Morgan is making no distinction between the happiness of the child in the Millennium and the child in heaven.

The streets of the city shall be full of boys and girls playing in the streets thereof.—Zech. 8:5

I draw your attention, first of all, to what this text reveals as the thought of God for the children. Let us imagine for a moment that we are not in London. We will transport ourselves to that

Kingdom which is to be, and to that city which the prophet saw. In that city we see, first, that God's ideal for the child is that the child shall play. . . . "The sucking child shall play on the hole of the asp, and the weaned child shall put his hand on the basilisk's den." [Isa. 11:8] That wonderful day when "the lion shall eat straw like the ox," and the wolf and the lamb shall lie down together in perfect peace, will be the child's playtime.

Have you ever taken a child to the zoological gardens, and have you ever been strangely perturbed by the child's deep anxiety to climb over the rails and get in amongst the polar bears? It is a Divine instinct. . . . "A little child shall lead them." It is the child at play, the child in the midst of nature, set there to play. . . . God's ideal for the child is that it shall play, and the characteristics of a little child at play are merriment, earnestness, pity, defense of the weak. Watch natural and healthy children at play and you will find that all these things are manifest in the midst of the play.

If I may carry this a little further I would say that God's ideal for the child is that it should play itself into its work. . . . In this age of collectivist thinking it is good sometimes to reassert the law of the individual, and every individual ought to be able to say concerning his or her life work, "To this end have I been born, and to this end am I come into the world." [John 18:37] That is true, not merely of the poets, dreamers and statesmen, but also of the men and women whom we sometimes insult by saying they do mean things [unimportant things]. There are no mean things if they come out of the capacity of the man who is doing them. If a little child learns its work through its play, all through the strenuous years you will find the man playing at his work. I do not mean playing with his work or doing it indifferently, but that it will be a delight to him. When work is what it ought to be in human life it is not a task set, not something done for profit merely, but something done for the sake of the thing done. I have been in a carpenter's shop and seen a man at the bench making some plain piece of furniture, and looking at it and touching it with love as he saw it developing under his hand. That is the real carpenter, brother to Jesus of Nazareth. If you find a man who loves his work he will have as secondary motive under it all the two things for which Paul says we are to work, the support of himself and his family, and to have something to give to him that is in need. Beyond that, work is done for the sake of the work, but children never come to that unless you give them their chance to play. You must begin with playtime for the children. That is God's ideal. . . .

If that be so, we may go yet a step further, and upon this foundation truth of God's purpose for the child and God's ideal for the child build the conditions of public life. This text is an index to the conditions of public life in the coming Kingdom. If in God's city boys and girls are to play in the streets of the city, then the streets of the city will be fit for the boys and girls to play in. Think what that means in the very simplest way. As Christ makes the child the type of character in His Kingdom, so the child comes to be the test of public life in the city of God. Everything in the life of the coming city will depend upon the little child. Everything will be carried forward in the interests of the little child. Among other things, the streets will be fit for children to play in. Said Isaiah, another of these prophets, "They shall not hurt nor destroy in all My holy mountain." [Isa. 11:9] What a city that will be where there will be nothing in the streets to harm little children, physically, mentally, or spiritually! When you have a city with streets fit for children you have a city with streets fit for adults. If the child is safe everyone is safe. Let us walk in imagination through some of the streets of the city of the King. I shall find nothing that can harm the child physically. In that city the drainage will be perfect, and the traffic and everything else will be watched by vigilant eyes for the sake of the children. You can dream your dreams around that. You tell me this is not the Gospel. Then what in the name of God is it? These children whom God loves and speaks of in the terms of playtime in His coming city are to be safe, and the measure in which children are safe in our streets today is the measure in which we have seen this ideal, and are working toward it.

Worth Thinking About

A city that is welcoming and safe for children is safe for anyone else. Do you live in a city that is safe for children, where they can walk to school and to the playground? Do you recall when most of our cities used to be this safe, safe for all of us to work and play? God cares intensely for children. Matthew 18:10 says: "Take heed that you do not despise one of these little ones, for I say to you that in heaven their angels always see the face of My Father who is in heaven." Another point to ponder: Heaven will be a place where our work will be as joyful the play of children. Imagine!

JESUS LOVES ME

Jesus loves me! He who died, Heaven's gate to open wide;

He will wash away my sin, let His little child come in.

Yes, Jesus loves me, yes, Jesus, loves me,

Yes, Jesus loves me, the Bible tells me so.

—Anna B. Warner

Prayer

DEAR FATHER, HELP ME TO GROW MORE CHILDLIKE IN MY FAITH AND LESS CHILDISH. HELP ME TO LOVE THE CHILDREN I MEET AND SEE YOU IN THEIR FACES. HELP ME TO FIT MYSELF AND THEM FOR YOUR HOME ABOVE WHERE OUR JOY WILL BE COMPLETE. AMEN.

WILL BEING IN HEAVEN HELP ME FIND OUT WHO I AM AS A PERSON?

Peter Kreeft

Dr. Peter Kreeft is a prolific author, and in reading this piece from *Heaven, the Heart's Deepest Longing* from Ignatius Press, 1989, you will be reminded that the age-old question of one's personal identity has always had an age-old answer. Dr. Kreeft, a professor of philosophy at Boston College, is used to tackling both practical issues and imaginary situations in books such as *Socrates Meets Jesus, Socrates Meets Machiavelli*, and *Socrates Meets Marx*. When he is not teaching at Boston College, he is lecturing, visiting other schools, and writing books. If *Heaven, the Heart's Deepest Longing* has a theme verse, it might well be Colossians 2:3: "In whom are hidden all the treasures of wisdom and knowledge." Kreeft reminds us that it is in losing ourselves to Christ that we find ourselves.

If heaven makes a difference to my identity, how do I find that difference? Human identity, unlike the identity of things in nature, is a problem, not a given. How do I find out who I am?

By the oldest and profoundest paradox of them all: "He who loses himself will find it." [Matt. 16:25] The most complete self-loss and self-finding is ecstasy, standing outside yourself. And the complete moment of standing outside yourself is the moment of death. Death is the "golden key" to my identity. Death is the door notionally of life but also of selfhood.

At death, God's love ravishes us right out of ourselves, sweeps us off our feet, off the ground, out of the earth, and out of the body. After death we are ravished even further: not only out of our bodies but out of our souls, our selves. Heaven is so self-forgetful that mystics who have experienced foretastes of it here often say they were absorbed into God, annihilated, or seen through as illusory.

This can't be literally true for the simple reason that only a self can be self-forgetful. Only one who exists can say, "I do not exist." No, the self God loved enough to create and redeem is not annihilated or illusory. It has found itself by completely forgetting itself; it has become a transparent window to God's light. Its mind thinks only God's thoughts and its will only God's will; so it can say like Christ: "I and the Father are one." [John 10:30] Yet they are also two: "The Father is greater than I." [John 14:28] "The two become one" [Gen. 2:24]—fleshly marriage dimly symbolizes our destiny, spiritual marriage to our God. . . .

The ecstasy of love is our training for heaven because it constructs the self that lives outside itself which is the only kind of self that can live in heaven. Beauty experiences something of heavenly ecstasy, but love creates it. (In fact, love even creates beauty, for to be loved is to become newly beautiful.) Beauty is the aroma of heavenly food; love is the eating of it. Beauty is God's silhouette; love is his life blood. Beauty is the shadow of heaven; love is its substance. . .

Every bit of love and beauty and truth that anyone ever experiences on earth is made in heaven and is a participation in heaven. For heaven is God's presence; and God is present in all goodness, all truth, and all beauty. God is not a truth, a good, or a beauty, but Goodness Itself and Truth Itself and Beauty Itself. He is neither a particular thing nor an abstract, universal quality, like "goodness in general." He is a concrete universal.

In God all goodness, truth, and beauty exist, coexist, meet, and are perfected.

Worth Thinking About

God intends that one day we will be perfectly like him when he completes his work in us after we die. In the meantime, here on earth he is working to perfect us or to make us completely whole. How can we best cooperate with him in this process? Have you lost yourself lately in being busy for God? Were you surprised by joy in the result?

TAKE TIME TO BE HOLY

Take time to be holy, speak oft with thy lord;
Abide in Him always, and feed on His Word.
Make friends with God's children; help those who are weak;
Forgetting in nothing His blessing to seek.
Take time to be holy, be calm in thy soul;
Each thought and each motive beneath His control;
Thus led by His Spirit to fountains of love,
Thou soon shalt be fitted for service above.

—W. D. Longstaff

Prayer

DEAR FATHER, HELP US TO BE SO PREOCCUPIED WITH YOU THAT WE FORGET THE DEMANDS OF EARTHLY BUSYNESS AND THE SELF-RIGHTEOUSNESS THAT SEPARATES US FROM YOU. THANK YOU THAT YOUR SPIRIT WORKS WITHIN US TO GROW IN GRACE AND LOVE FOR JESUS. AMEN.

What Will It Be Like to Be Free from the Temptation to Sin?

St. Augustine

Temptations are a commonplace condition of the earthly life. It is hard to turn around and not run into a commandment we are tempted to break for the sake of convenience and selfish living. Thus, one of the great benefits of heaven will be that at last we will be free from temptation, for we will not even find any part of our nature attracted to sin. That will be our entire and perfect sanctification. This excerpt is taken from *The City of God*, book twenty-two, and comments on the greater freedom our wills will have when there is no longer temptation to sin.

Who can measure the happiness of heaven, where no evil at all can touch us, no good will be out of reach; where life is to be one long laud extolling God, who will be all in all; where there will be no weariness to call for rest, no need to call for toil, no place for any energy but praise. Of this I am assured whenever I read or hear the sacred song: "Blessed are they that dwell in thy house, O Lord: they shall praise thee for ever and ever." [Ps. 84:2-3] Every fiber and organ of our imperishable body will play its part in the praising of God.

On earth these varied organs have each a special function, but, in heaven, function will be swallowed up in felicity, in the perfect certainty of an untroubled everlastingness of joy. Even those muted notes in the diapason [harmonious sound—Ed.] of the human organ, which I mentioned earlier, will swell into a great hymn of praise to the supreme Artist who has fashioned us, within and without, in every fiber, and who, by this and every other element of a magnificent and marvelous Order, will ravish our minds with spiritual beauty.

These movements of our bodies will be of such unimaginable beauty that I dare not say more than this: There will be such poise, such grace, such beauty as become a place where nothing unbecoming can be found. Wherever the spirit wills, there, in a flash, will the body be. Nor will the spirit ever will anything unbecoming either to itself or to the body.

In heaven, all glory will be true glory, since no one could ever err in praising too little or too much. True honor will never be denied where due, never be given where undeserved, and, since none but the worthy are permitted there, no one will unworthily ambition [strive for—Ed.] glory. Perfect peace will reign, since nothing in ourselves or in any others could disturb this peace. The promised reward of virtue will be the best and the greatest of all possible prizes—the very Giver of virtue Himself, for that is what the Prophet meant: "I will be your God and you shall be my people." [Ex. 6:7] God will be the source of every satisfaction, more than any heart can rightly crave, more than life and health, food and wealth, glory and honor, peace and every good—so that God, as St. Paul said, "may be all in all." [1 Cor. 15:28] He will be the consummation of all our desiring—the object of our unending vision, of our unlessening love, of our unwearying praise. And in this gift of vision, this response of love, this paean of praise, all alike will share, as all will share in everlasting life.

But, now, who can imagine, let alone describe, the ranks upon ranks of rewarded saints, to be graded, undoubtedly, according to their variously merited honor and glory. Yet, there will be no envy of the lower for the higher, as there is no· envy of angel for archangel—for this is one of the great blessednesses of this blessed City. The less rewarded will be linked in perfect peace with the more highly favored, but lower could not more long for higher than a finger, in the ordered integration of a body, could want to be an eye. The less endowed will have the high endowment of longing for nothing loftier than their lower gifts.

The souls in bliss will still possess the freedom of will, though sin will have no power to tempt them. They will be more free than ever-so free, in fact, from all delight in sinning as to find, in not sinning, an unfailing source of joy. By the freedom which was given to the first man, who was constituted in rectitude, he could choose either to sin or not to sin; in eternity, freedom is that more potent freedom which makes all sin impossible. Such freedom, of course, is a gift of God, beyond the power of nature to achieve. For, it is one thing to be God, another to be a sharer in the divine nature. God, by His nature, cannot sin, but a mere sharer in His nature must receive from God such immunity from sin. It was proper that, in the process of divine endowment, the first step should be a freedom not to sin, and the last a freedom even from the power to sin. The first gift made merit possible; the second is a part of man's reward. Our nature, when it was free to sin, did sin. It took a greater grace to lead us to that larger liberty which frees us from the very power to sin. Just as the immortality that Adam lost by his sin was, at first, a mere possibility of avoiding death, but, in heaven, becomes the impossibility of death, so free will was, at first, a mere possibility of avoiding sin, but, in heaven, becomes an utter inability to sin.

Our will will be as ineradicably rooted in rectitude and love as in beatitude. It is true that, with Adam's sin, we lost our right to grace and glory, but, with our right, we did not lose our longing to be happy. And, as for freedom, can we think that God Himself, who certainly cannot sin, is therefore without freedom? The conclusion is that, in the everlasting City, there will remain in each and all of us an inalienable freedom of the will, emancipating us from every evil and filling us with every good, rejoicing in the inexhaustible beatitude of everlasting happiness, unclouded by the memory of any sin or of sanction suffered, yet with no forgetfulness of our redemption nor any loss of gratitude for our Redeemer.

Worth Thinking About

Heaven, the home of transformed hearts, will be remarkable for its lack of so many things to which we have become accustomed. Can you imagine the time when you will not succumb to temptation, a temporary enjoyment of wrongdoing, an indifference to those around you, anger, or a disappointment in yourself when you do not come out on top? How strange and marvelous it will be to cheer when others succeed and to rejoice at our humble place in the scheme of things.

HOW BLESSED IS HE WHOSE TRESPASS

How blest is he whose trespass has freely been forgiven,

Whose sin is wholly covered before the sight of heaven,

Blest be to whom Jehovah imputeth not his sin,

Who hath a guileless spirit, whose heart is true within.

—Anonymous

Prayer

DEAR FATHER, THANK YOU FOR THE FUTURE THAT AWAITS ME WHEN I SHALL EVER BE FREE FROM TEMPTATION BECAUSE ALL THAT I WANT I HAVE FOUND IN YOU. HELP ME START THIS JOURNEY OF PRAISE NOW AS I WORSHIP AND SERVE YOU FROM DAY TO DAY. AMEN.

How Can I Enjoy a Taste of Heaven in My Everyday Walk?

F. B. Meyer (1847-1929)

F. B. Meyer , a Baptist minister and friend of evangelist D. L. Moody, held several pastorates in England but also spoke widely in the United States. An educated man, he graduated from the University of London and wrote over forty books, including *Ephesians: A Devotional Commentary*. His association with so-called "higher living" Christianity is evident in this excerpt from *Ephesians*. Note that Meyer is not talking about having a "Heaven now" on earth but of having a heaven-like life here and now.

In his conversation with Nicodemus, while the night-breeze played over the sleeping city, coming and going as it would, our Lord spoke of Himself as being already in heaven. His bodily presence was evidently in the chamber of that house in Jerusalem, robed in the simple peasant garb which his mother had spun for Him; but in spirit, He was much more really in heaven than there. So, according to the teaching of the apostle Paul, the Church, consisting of such as believe in Christ, is really less a denizen of earth than of those heavenly places which have been entered by her Lord. They are not heaven, but heaven-like.

All Spiritual Blessings Are Stored There. (Ephesians 1:3) Human speech could never tell the infinite variety of blessings which are required for the life of the saints. Grace to endure what

God sends or permits, as well as to do what He commands. So destitute are we of natural qualities and powers that we need to receive all things that pertain to life and godliness. Everything that Christ asks of us must be received from Him before it can be yielded to Him. It is therefore a source of deep heart's-ease to learn that God has stored in Jesus every spiritual blessing. As all colour lies hidden in sunlight, waiting to be drawn off by the flowers, so does help for every time of need reside in Christ.

The tense denotes a definite past act. The apostle does not say that God does or will bless; but that He has blessed. He carries us back into the eternal ages, in which we were created in Christ, so far as the eternal purpose is concerned, and assures us that then every conceivable blessing which we should need in our earthly pilgrimage was stored up in Christ Jesus our Lord. We have not therefore to plead for these things, as though God were unwilling to give; but humbly and reverently to lay claim to them by faith. All things are yours, O Christian soul; by which you may become partaker of the Divine nature, and escape the corruption that is in the world by lust.

But since these spiritual blessings are in the heavenly places, we must live upon that plane. This is where so many mistake. They know that all the land is theirs; but they do not put their foot down upon it. We cannot inherit the treasures of the everlasting hills, whilst we are satisfied with the heavy air of the valleys. Our daily life must be spent in fellowship with the living Jesus; our thought and heart must not only ascend to Him, but continually dwell with Him; we must experimentally sit in the heavenly places ere we can claim or possess the things which God hath prepared for them that love Him. . . .

We need not, therefore, anxiously inquire what "the heavenly places" are, or where. It is enough to know that they are where Jesus is, and that they are open to us, just in proportion as we live in communion with the Lord. Abide in Him, and you are by necessity an inhabitant of these heavenly places, wherever your earthly lot may be cast. They are the hallowed meeting ground, where the saints of earth come to the spirits of the just made perfect. It was of them that Bunyan spoke, when, describing the land of Beulah, he said, "Here they were within sight of the city they were going to; also here met them some of the inhabitants thereof, for in this land the Shining Ones commonly walked, because it was upon the borders of heaven. . . ."

We sit there in the purpose of God. (Eph. 2:6)

What Canaan was to the Jewish people, that the heavenly places are to us. When the twelve stones were taken from the bed of the Jordan and placed on the hither side, the whole people were deemed to have entered upon the possession of their inheritance; though as a matter of fact, two-and-a-half tribes had elected to settle on the farther side, and their wives and children would probably never cross the Jordan at all. [Josh. 4:1-9] So when Jesus passed to the throne we passed with Him.

Was He raised? So were we. Was He made to sit at the Father's right hand? That is our place. Was every foe made his footstool? Then not one of them can overcome us so long as we are in abiding fellowship with our risen Lord. If the "together" of the inner life is maintained, the "together" of victory is secure. Oh, to tread in the power of the Holy Ghost on these high places!

Worth Thinking About

Sometime this week you might want to take a moment to think about how Christ's death and sacrifice for our sins helps us to live a heaven-like life now. How heavenly can we make life now while still dealing with trials and temptations? Why not share your insights with someone else and pass on the blessing?

MARCHING TO ZION

Come we that love the Lord, and let our joys be known,
Join in a song with sweet accord, join in a song with sweet accord,
And thus surround the throne, and thus surround the throne.
We're marching to Zion, beautiful, beautiful Zion;
We're marching upward to Zion, the beautiful city of God.

—Isaac Watts

Prayer

DEAR FATHER, HELP US TO WALK IN THE LIGHT OF HEAVEN THAT WE MAY DO EARTHLY GOOD AS A WITNESS TO YOU. HELP US TO REALIZE THAT HEAVEN IS OUR TRUE HOME AND MAKE US INTENSELY DISSATISFIED WITH ANYTHING LESS THAN WANTING TO BE THERE. AMEN.

Do We Long for God's Heavenly Rewards?

Clement (?-101)

Although we know little about Clement (who is sometimes called Clement of Rome; for it is thought that he was a leading bishop there), he was perhaps consecrated into ministry by the apostle Peter himself. We also know that he was a practical man given to heavenly matters. He is regarded as Clement I by Catholics who honor him as the second Pope after Peter. In this letter, Clement is directing the still fractious church at Corinth (remember the apostle Paul's letters?) to make peace among its members and keep the principles of heaven before their eyes. This message is excerpted from *The Apostolic Fathers* issued by Moody Classics in 2009.

For the Creator and Master of the universe himself rejoices in his works. Thus by his almighty power he established the heavens and by his inscrutable wisdom he arranged them. He separated the land from the water surrounding it and fixed it upon the sure foundation of his own will. By his decree he brought into existence the living creatures which roam on it; and after creating the sea and the creatures which inhabit it, he fixed its boundaries by his power. Above all, with his holy and pure hands he formed man, his outstanding and greatest achievement, stamped with his own image. For this is what God said: "Let us make man in our own image and likeness. And God made man: male and female he created." [Gen. 1:1, 2:23] And so, when he had finished all this, he praised it and blessed it and said, "Increase and multiply." [Gen. 1:22] We should observe that all the righteous have been adorned with good deeds and the very Lord adorns himself with good deeds and rejoices. Since, then, we have this example, we should unhesitatingly give ourselves to his will, and put all our effort into acting uprightly.

The good laborer accepts the bread he has earned with his head held high; the lazy and negligent workman cannot look his employer in the face. We must, then, be eager to do good; for everything comes from Him. For he warns us: "See, the Lord is coming. He is bringing his reward with him, to pay each one according to his work." [Matt. 16:27] He bids us, therefore, to believe on him with all our heart, and not to be slack or negligent in "every good deed." [Titus 2:14] He should be the basis of our boasting and assurance. We should be subject to his will. We should note how the whole throng of his angels stands ready to serve his will. For Scripture says: "Ten thousand times ten thousand stood by him, and thousands of thousands ministered to him and cried out: Holy, holy, holy is the Lord of Hosts: all creation is full of his glory." [Isa. 6:3]

We too, then, should gather together for worship in concord and mutual trust, and earnestly beseech him as it were with one mouth, that we may share in his great and glorious promises. For he says, "Eye has not seen and ear has not heard and man's heart has not conceived what he has prepared for those who patiently wait for him. . . ." [1 Cor. 2:9]

How blessed and amazing are God's gifts, dear friends! Life with immortality, splendor with righteousness, truth with confidence, faith with assurance, self-control with holiness! And all these things are within our comprehension. . . .

Through him we fix our gaze on the heights of heaven. In him we see mirrored God's pure and transcendent face. Through him the eyes of our hearts have been opened. Through him our foolish and darkened understanding springs up to the light. Through him the Master has willed that we should taste immortal knowledge.

—∞∞∞—

Worth Thinking About

"We must, then, be eager to do good; for everything comes from Him," Clement says. And he is thinking about the rewards laid up in heaven for those who fear God and do His will. Have you been investing your treasures in heaven—where you can't lose what is secured there?

LO, FROM VESSELS EARTHEN ONLY

Earthen vessels, marred, unsightly,

But the treasures as of old,

Fresh from glory, gleaming brightly,

Heav'n's undimmed, unchanging gold.

God's own hand the vessel filling

From the glory far above,

Longing hearts forever stilling

With those riches of His love.

—Frances Bevan

Prayer

DEAR FATHER, HELP ME TO SEE HOW SURE HEAVENLY INVESTMENTS ARE AND HELP ME TO KNOW THAT THE REWARDS OF HEAVEN ARE FAR MORE THAN THE REWARDS OF EARTH. HELP ME TO GATHER WITH OTHERS IN YOUR NAME THAT WE MIGHT STRENGTHEN EACH OTHER IN OUR WORK. AMEN.

How May I Receive the Gift of Heaven in a Way That Pleases Him?

Andrew Murray (1828-1917)

The Rev. Andrew Murray had a wide influence in both England and America because of his popular devotional writings that emphasized yielding oneself to Christ. Born in South Africa, he continued to minister there after having a Scottish and Dutch education. For him humility was supreme virtue and a foretaste of the divine life and an essential attitude for fitting oneself for heaven. Murray specialized in the topic of what made for sanctified living and became a specialist about it. His work remains very influential for those seeking the keys to abundant living. His book *Humility* was published by Anson D. F. Randolph & Co. in 1895. This excerpt is from the chapter "Humility: The Glory of the Creature."

Thou art worthy, O Lord, to receive glory and honour and power; for thou hast   created all things, and for thy pleasure they are and were created.—Rev. 4:11

When God created the universe, it was with the one object of making the creature partaker of His perfection and blessedness, and so showing forth in it the glory of His love and wisdom and power. God wished to reveal Himself in and through created beings by communicating to them as much of His own goodness and glory as they were capable of receiving. But this communication was not a giving to the creature something which it could possess in itself, a certain life or goodness, of which it had the charge and disposal. By no means. But as God is the ever-living, ever-present, ever-acting One, who upholds all things by the word of His power, and in whom all things exist, the relation of the creature to God could only be one of unceasing, absolute, universal dependence. As truly as God by His power once created, so truly by that same power must God every moment maintain. The creature has not only to look back to the origin and first beginning of existence, and acknowledge that it there owes everything to God; its chief care, its highest virtue, its only happiness, now and through all eternity, is to present itself an empty vessel, in which God can dwell and manifest His power and goodness.

The life God bestows is imparted not once for all, but each moment continuously, by the unceasing operation of His mighty power. Humility, the place of entire dependence on God, is, from the very nature of things, the first duty and the highest virtue of the creature, and the root of every virtue.

And so pride, or the loss of this humility, is the root of every sin and evil. It was when the now fallen angels began to look upon themselves with self-complacency that they were led to disobedience, and were cast down from the light of heaven into outer darkness. Even so it was, when the serpent breathed the poison of his pride—the desire to be as God, into the hearts of our first parents—they too fell from their high estate into all the wretchedness in which man is now sunk. In heaven and earth, pride, self-exaltation, is the gate and the birth, and the curse, of hell.

Hence it follows that nothing can be our redemption, but the restoration of the lost humility, the original and only true relation of the creature to its God. And so Jesus came to bring humility back to earth, to make us partakers of it, and by it to save us.

In heaven He humbled Himself to become man. The humility we see in Him possessed Him in heaven; it brought Him, He brought it, from there. Here on earth "He humbled Himself, and became obedient unto death"; His humility gave His death its value, and so became our redemption. And now the salvation He imparts is nothing less and nothing else than a communication of His own life and death, His own disposition and spirit, His own humility, as the ground and root of His relation to God and His redeeming work. Jesus Christ took the place and fulfilled the destiny of man, as a creature, by His life of perfect humility. His humility is our salvation. His salvation is our humility.

And so the life of the saved ones, of the saints, must needs bear this stamp of deliverance from sin, and full restoration to their original state; their whole relation to God and man marked by an all-pervading humility. Without this there can be no true abiding in God's presence, or experience of His favor and the power of His Spirit; without this no abiding faith, or love or joy or strength. Humility is the only soil in which the graces root; the lack of humility is the sufficient explanation of every defect and failure. Humility is not so much a grace or virtue along with others; it is the root of all, because it alone takes the right attitude before God, and allows Him as God to do all.

God has so constituted us as reasonable beings, that the truer the insight into the real nature or the absolute need of a command, the readier and fuller will be our obedience to it. The call to humility has been too little regarded in the Church because its true nature and importance has been too little apprehended. It is not a something which we bring to God, or He bestows; it is simply the sense of entire nothingness, which comes when we see how truly God is all, and in which we make way for God to be all. When the creature realizes that this is the true nobility, and consents to be with his will, his mind, and his affections, the form, the vessel in which the life and glory of God are to work and manifest themselves, he sees that humility is simply acknowledging the truth of his position as creature, and yielding to God His place.

Worth Thinking About

If we love God, we know that humility naturally arises out of appreciating what we have received from Him. His riches to us include all the riches of heaven, yet we must be aware that the world is always throwing out for display its glittering attractions. The trouble is, the attractions just don't last, and they can never satisfy. Yet how difficult it is to maintain this truth in our hearts! Let us pursue humility and resist material desires.

WHEN I SURVEY THE WONDROUS CROSS

When I survey the wondrous cross on which the Prince of Glory died,
My richest gain I count but loss, and pour contempt on all my pride.
Forbid it, Lord, that I should boast, save in the death of Christ my God:
All the vain things that charm me most, I sacrifice them to His blood.

—Isaac Watts

Prayer

DEAR FATHER, HELP ME LEARN FROM CHRIST'S HUMILITY AND BE SELF-FORGETFUL FOR THE SAKE OF OTHERS. HELP ME TO LEARN AS PAUL DID TO BE CONTENT WITH WHAT I HAVE, KNOWING HOW TO REJOICE WHEN I ABOUND IN THINGS AND WHEN I DO NOT. AMEN.

WHAT CAN I DO TO BRING A TOUCH OF HEAVEN TO EARTH?

Henry Drummond (1851-1897)

Henry Drummond was a Scottish minister who participated in evangelistic campaigns across the United Kingdom with D. L. Moody. He is best known today for his devotional classic *The Greatest Thing in the World*, a meditation on 1 Corinthians chapter thirteen. This small book has sold over 12 million copies and is still in print. Drummond believed that the holy City of God was something not only to be expected in the life to come but was also to be enacted now as Christians worked to extend God's kingdom through all the earth. This sermon was published by James Potts and Company in 1893 and is titled "I Saw the City."

⚭

> I, John, saw the Holy City, New Jerusalem, Coming down from God out of Heaven. . . . And I saw no Temple therein. . . . And His servants shall serve Him; and they shall see His Face; and His Name shall be written on their foreheads.—Rev. 21:2-4

Two very startling things arrest us in John's vision of the future. The first is that the likeliest thing to Heaven he could think of was a City; the second, that there was no Church in that City.

Almost nothing more revolutionary could be said, even to the modern world, in the name of religion. No Church—that is the defiance of religion; a City—that is the antipodes of

Heaven. Yet John combines these contradictions in one daring image, and holds up to the world the picture of a City without a Church as his ideal of the heavenly life.

By far the most original thing here is the simple conception of Heaven as a City. The idea of religion without a Church—"I saw no Temple therein"—is anomalous enough; but the association of the blessed life with a City—the one place in the world from which Heaven seems most far away—is something wholly new in religious thought. No other religion which has a Heaven ever had a Heaven like this. The Greek, if he looked forward at all, awaited the Elysian Fields; the Eastern sought Nirvana. All other Heavens have been Gardens, Dreamlands—passivities more or less aimless. Even to the majority among ourselves Heaven is a siesta and not a City. It remained for John to go straight to the other extreme and select the citadel of the world's fever, the ganglion of its unrest, the heart and focus of its most strenuous toil, as the framework for his ideal of the blessed life.

The Heaven of Christianity is different from all other Heavens, because the religion of Christianity is different from all other religions. Christianity is the religion of Cities. It moves among real things. Its sphere is the street, the market-place, the working-life of the world.

And what interests one for the present in John's vision is not so much what it reveals of a Heaven beyond, but what it suggests of the nature of the heavenly life in this present world. Find out what a man's Heaven is—no matter whether it be a dream or a reality, no matter whether it refer to an actual Heaven or to a Kingdom of God to be realized on earth—and you pass by an easy discovery to what his religion is; and herein lies one value at least of this allegory. It is a touchstone for Christianity, a test for the solidity or the insipidity of one's religion, for the wholesomeness or the fatuousness of one's faith, for the usefulness or the futility of one's life. For this vision of the City marks off in lines which no eye can mistake the true area which the religion of Christ is meant to inhabit, and announces for all time the real nature of the saintly life.

City life is human life at its intensest, man in his most real relations. And the nearer one draws to reality, the nearer one draws to the working sphere of religion. Wherever real life is, there Christ goes. And He goes there, not only because the great need lies there, but because there is found, so to speak, the raw material with which Christianity works—the life of man. To do something with this, to infuse something into this, to save and inspire and sanctify this, the actual working life of the world, is what He came for. Without human life to act upon, without the relations of men with one another, of master with servant, husband with wife, buyer with seller, creditor with debtor, there is no such thing as Christianity. With actual things, with Humanity in its everyday dress, with the traffic of the streets, with gates and houses, with work and wages, with sin and poverty, with these things, and all the things and all the relations and all the people of the City, Christianity has to do and has more to do than with anything else. To conceive of the Christian religion as itself a thing—a something which can exist apart from life; to think of it as something added on to being, something kept in a separate compartment called the soul, as an extra accomplishment like music, or a special talent like art, is totally to misapprehend its nature. It is that which fills all compartments. It is that which makes the whole life music and every separate action a work of art. Take away action and it is not. Take away people, houses, streets, character, and it ceases to be. Without these there may be sentiment, or rapture, or adoration, or superstition; there may even be religion, but there can never be the religion of the Son of Man.

Worth Thinking About

Yes, Scripture does say that we will dwell in the "new Jerusalem," a city, yet when we see the cities with which we are familiar, do we wonder how they could ever be made to show forth the glory of heaven? How do you think of heaven? What would a perfect city be like? How can the spread of the gospel now be a vision for the future in which the world and all who live in it will be renewed in true righteousness and holiness (Eph. 4:24)?

LET ALL THE WORLD IN EVERY CORNER SING

Let all the world in every corner sing: My God and King!

The heav'ns are not too high His praise may thither fly

The earth is not too low His praises there may grow,

Let all the world in every corner sing: My God and King!

—George Herbert

Prayer

DEAR FATHER, HOLY IS YOUR NAME. MAY YOUR KINGDOM COME AND YOUR WILL BE DONE ON EARTH AS IT IS IN HEAVEN. HELP US TO SUPPORT CHRISTIAN WORK THAT GOES ON IN OUR CITIES NOW. HELP US TO PRAY FOR THE HOMELESS AND LEARN HOW TO BEST HELP THOSE WHO ARE UN-CHURCHED IN OUR CITIES. AMEN.

How Does the Allegory of Sarah and Hagar Reveal Aspects of Heaven?

Dale Moody (1915-1991)

Dr. Dale Moody was an influential theologian and teacher who lectured in systematic theology for over forty years at Southern Baptist Theological Seminary in Louisville, Kentucky. His basic doctrinal book was *The Word of Truth*, published by Wm. B. Eerdmans in 1981. The excerpt is taken from his standard work on last things called *The Hope of Glory*, published by the same company in 1964. Dr. Moody here looks at one of the Bible's most famous allegories about receiving the inheritance of heaven through God-ordained methods rather than through human means. Who would have thought that the story of Sarah and Hagar would teach us of heavenly truths?

The tension between the earthly symbol and the heavenly reality became taut after the death of Jesus in Jerusalem. Even before the fall of the city in A.D. 70, Paul put the two in strong contrast in his polemic against what he considered "another gospel" (Gal. 1:7). With the figure of God as Father of both his Son Jesus Christ, and his sons, the true Christians, he describes how we are delivered from slavery to sonship by God first sending forth His Son from heaven to earth, and then sending forth His Spirit into the hearts of His sons (4:1-7). Paul is alarmed lest the process be reversed and they turn from sonship back to slavery "to the weak and beggarly elemental spirits" (4:8-11). This is his travail for their souls (4:12-20).

The Allegory of the Two Women. The allegory of the two women, Hagar and Sarah as the two covenants, follows (Gal. 4:21-31), and the system of slavery advocated by Judaism is represented by Hagar, Sinai, and the present Jerusalem. But there is the heavenly Jerusalem, and the Jerusalem above, which is free: "she is our mother" (4:26) With God as our Father and the heavenly Jerusalem as our mother we are free, and we should "stand fast therefore" and "not submit to a yoke of slavery" (5:1). Sarah has become the symbol of freedom as Hagar was the symbol of slavery. . . .

The heavenly Jerusalem is now "above," the abode of Christ. That is why Paul points away from human tradition to this heavenly realm of reality when he says: "If then you have been raised with Christ, seek the things that are above, where Christ is, seated at the right hand of God. Set your minds on things above, not on things that are on earth" (Col. 3:1f.). The Church is on earth, but she is called to give attention to the things of heaven. She may worship *with* the angels, but she must not worship the angels and become in bondage again to "the elemental spirits of the universe" (2:20). . . .

The Christian does give his supreme allegiance to this heavenly realm above. Of those who mind earthly things it is said: "Their end is destruction, their god is the belly, and they glory in their shame, with minds set on earthly things" (Phil. 3:19). Of us who set our minds on heavenly things it is very different: "Our commonwealth is in heaven, and from it we await a Savior, the Lord Jesus Christ, who will change our lowly body like unto his glorious body, by the power which enables him even to subject all things to himself" (3:20). Heaven is our home town, our native land.

*W*orth Thinking About

We who are of Sarah are the children of the promise because the child through Hagar was a merely human plan (see all of Galatians 4:21-31). Do we order our plans by His promises or His promises by our plans? If it is the latter, we cannot achieve God's good ends. Do you take Scripture just as it is or do you try to make it fit your own circumstances?

STANDING ON THE PROMISES

Standing on the promises that cannot fail
When the howling storms of doubt and fear assail;
By the living world of God I shall prevail—
Standing on the promises of God.
Standing on the promises of Christ the Lord,
Bound to Him eternally by love's strong cord;
Overcoming daily with the Spirit's sword,
Standing on the promises of God.

—Russell K. Carter

*P*rayer

DEAR FATHER, AS WE WAIT FOR JESUS TO COME AND TAKE US HOME, HELP US TO BE BUSY FOR HIM. MAY OTHERS SEE CHRIST WHEN THEY SEE US DEPENDING ON YOUR PROMISES, AND HELP US TO CLEARLY UNDERSTAND THOSE PROMISES. AMEN.

How Does God's Witness in Nature Suggest the Reality of Heaven?

Alister E. McGrath

Dr. Alister McGrath is a leading British theologian and professor who took two doctorates at Oxford University, one in Molecular Biophysics and the other in theology. He has taught at both Oxford and Cambridge Universities and is currently Professor of Ministry, Theology and Education at King's College, London. The author of over thirty books, McGrath here discusses what we can know of heaven through "natural revelation," or the witness of nature, that demonstrates eternal truth about God. How do you understand the Bible when it says:

The heavens declare the glory of God; and the firmament shows His handiwork. Day unto day utters speech, and night unto night reveals knowledge. There is no speech nor language where their voice is not heard. Their line has gone out through all the earth, and their words to the end of the world (Ps. 19:1-4).

What do you think nature can tell us of heaven? Have you had experiences in nature that cause you to believe in a creator of what you see?

This excerpt is taken from McGrath's 2003 book *A Brief History of Heaven*, published by Blackwell of Oxford.

∞∞∞

One of the most fundamental themes of Christian worldview is that humanity has been created "in the image of God" (Genesis 1:27), with the endowed capacity to relate to the God who thus created them, and who subsequently redeemed them in Christ. It is not surprising that many theologians—among them, Augustine of Hippo—should draw attention to the consequent human sense of longing, interpreting this as the memory of a lost paradise and the anticipation of that paradise regained in heaven. As Anselm of Canterbury pointed out during the eleventh century, God purposefully created humanity with the explicit intention of leading them into eternal blessedness and has therefore made them yearn for that final goal.

Yet the external world of nature also offers a rich tapestry of hints and rumors of a lost paradise and its potential restoration. In an article entitled "Nature as a Parable," Malcolm Muggeridge points out how a Christian understanding of creation is intimately linked to the notion of nature as a sign of the transcendent, pointing beyond itself conveying something of its creator.

Everything that happens to us or in connection with us, all the happenings in the world, great and small, the whole exterior phenomenon of nature and of life—all that amounts to God speaking to us, sending out messages in code, and faith is the key whereby we may decipher them. It sounds very simple, but it's somehow difficult to convey exactly . . . Nature is speaking to us. It is a parable of life itself, a revelation of fearful symmetry.

Paradise is thus not merely a misty memory of an event at the dawn of history, nor a distant promised hope; it is something that engages the imagination here and now partly through the promptings of a richly signed natural order, and partly through the divinely inspired human yearning for transcendence [eternity—Ed. note]. . . .

The longing for heaven that is evoked by nature is held to rest on the anticipation of seeing the creator of the world, who may be dimly glimpsed through the wonders of the created order.

The American theologian and preacher Jonathan Edwards made this point in his famous sermon "The Christian Pilgrim," preached in September 1733:

God is the highest good of the reasonable creature, and the enjoyment of him is the only happiness with which our souls can be satisfied. To go to heaven fully to enjoy God, is infinitely better than the most pleasant accommodations here. Fathers and mothers, husbands, wives, children, or the company of earthly friends, are but shadows. But the enjoyment of God is the substance. These are but scattered beams, but God is the sun. These are but streams, but God is the fountain. These are but drops, but God is the ocean.

Worth Thinking About

Few theologians teach that the revelation of God in nature is a perfect witness. After all, the fall of man also has to be explained, and the apostle Paul says that the whole of creation is in "bondage" to the effects of sin. Hence, most Christian thinkers believe that nature gives an imperfect witness to the glory of God. Why do you think that some insurance companies refer to natural disasters as "acts of God," but that you hear less of the beauty of a sunset as being declared an act of God? Which way of looking at things do you find within yourself?

I SING THE MIGHTY POWER OF GOD

I sing the mighty power of God that made the mountains rise,

That spread the flowing seas abroad and built the lofty skies.

I sing the wisdom that ordained the sun to rule the day;

The moon shines full at God's command and all the stars obey.

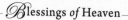

I sing the goodness of the Lord, who filled the earth with food,

Who formed the creatures through the Word and
then pronounced them good.

Lord, how Thy wonders are displayed where'er I turn my eye,

If I survey the ground I tread or gaze upon the sky.

—Isaac Watts

Prayer

DEAR FATHER, GREAT ARE YOUR WORKS AND MANY ASTONISH US WHILE, IN OUR DULLNESS, WE MISS MUCH THAT SHOUTS OF YOUR GLORY. MAY YOU AWAKEN OUR EYES THAT WE MAY BEHOLD THE WONDERFUL THINGS YOU HAVE MADE, AND MAY THEY CREATE IN US A HUNGER FOR THAT WHICH IS PERFECT AND CAN BE FOUND ONLY IN HEAVEN YOUR DWELLING PLACE. AMEN.

Is My Longing for Heaven a Clue That Heaven Is Really There?

C. S. Lewis (1898-1963)

Dr. C. S. Lewis, a lifelong student and teacher of English literature at Oxford University, was a romantic by inclination and put much stock in an experience that he felt was shared by people of every culture. The experience that he felt was significant was what he called "immortal" longings or yearnings for something joyful that lies just beyond reach. The happiest people, Lewis felt, were those who finally came to realize that this longing was pointing them to the God who made heaven and earth and created this longing in them.

The book *Mere Christianity* came out from Geoffrey Bles Publishers of London during World War II. Three separate pamphlets of broadcast talks made over the BBC radio were gathered in 1944 to make the book. Since that time *Mere Christianity* has never been out of print and has had an enormous influence as an apologetic for Christianity. This excerpt is from the chapter "Hope."

The Christian Way—The Christian says, "Creatures are not born with desires unless satisfaction for those desires exists. A baby feels hunger: well, there is such a thing as food. A duckling wants to swim: well, there is such a thing as water. Men feel sexual desire: well, there is such a thing as sex. If I find in myself a desire which no experience in this world can satisfy, the most probable explanation is that I was made for another world. If none of my earthly pleasures satisfy it, that does not prove that the universe is a fraud. Probably earthly pleasures were never meant to satisfy it, but only to arouse it, to suggest the real thing. If that is so, I must take care, on the one hand, never to despise, or be unthankful for, these earthly blessings, and on the other, never to mistake them for the something else of which they are only a kind of copy, or echo, or mirage. I must keep alive in myself the desire for my true country, which I shall not find till after death; I must never let it get snowed under or turned aside: I must make it the main object of life to press on to that other country and to help others to do the same."

There is no need to be worried by facetious people who try to make the Christian hope of "Heaven" ridiculous by saying they do not want "to spend eternity playing harps." The answer to such people is that if they cannot understand books written for grown-ups, they should not talk about them. All the scriptural imagery (harps, crowns, gold, etc.) is, of course, a merely symbolical attempt to express the inexpressible. Musical instruments are mentioned because for many people (not all) music is the thing known in the present life which most strongly suggests ecstasy and infinity. Crowns are mentioned to suggest the fact that those who are united with God in eternity share His splendour and power and joy. Gold is mentioned to suggest the timelessness of Heaven (gold does not rust) and the preciousness of it. People who take these symbols literally might as well think that when Christ told us to be like doves, He meant that we were to lay eggs. . . .

Worth Thinking About

Have you ever felt longings for things that promise satisfaction but never seem to give it? On television people are often shown as being happy over buying a new car or drinking a good beer. Have you ever tried to buy happiness? Were you satisfied with the result? How would you describe an immortal longing? Have you ever had one? If you have time, reread this from Lewis again and think about it.

WHEN I SURVEY THE WONDROUS CROSS

Forbid it, Lord, that I should boast save in the death of Christ,
my God:

All the vain things that charm me most I sacrifice them to His blood.

See, from His head, His hands, His feet,
sorrow and love flow mingled down:

Did e'er such love and sorrow meet,
or thorns compose so rich a crown?

—Isaac Watts

Prayer

DEAR FATHER, HELP ME TO PAY ATTENTION TO MY IMMORTAL LONGINGS AND KNOW THAT THEY ARE REALLY FULFILLED IN YOU ALONE. AND WHEN I MEET OTHER PEOPLE WHO AREN'T SATISFIED OR WHO SEEM TO BE LOOKING FOR SOMETHING MORE, HELP ME TO INTRODUCE THEM TO YOU. AMEN.

How Do the Heavens Declare the Glory of God?

Hannah More (1745-1833)

Hannah More was a social and educational reformer and a philanthropist who founded many Sunday schools and campaigned for the abolition of the slave trade in England. Additionally, she was a successful writer who enjoyed considerable influence in her day. In this selection taken from *The Pilgrims* (an allegory) she suggests that an actual study of the stars might clear one's eyes to see the greatness of the things above and the smallness of the things of earth. "The heavens declare the glory of God; and the firmament shows His handiwork" (Ps. 19:1).

⊗⊗⊗

But none did this [set aside zeal for owning the things of earth—Ed.] with much zeal or acceptance but those who had acquired a habit of overlooking "the things below," and who also, by the constant use of the telescope [faith], had gotten their natural weak and dim sight so strengthened as to be able to discern pretty distinctly the nature of "the things above." The habit of fixing their eyes on these glories made all the shining trifles which compose the mass of "things below," at last appear in their own smallness. For it was in this case particularly true, that things are only big or little by comparison; and there was no other way of making "the things below" appear as small as they really were, but by comparing them, by means of the telescope, with "the things above."

But I observed that the false judgment of the pilgrims ever kept pace with their wrong practices; for those who kept their eyes fastened on "the things below," were reckoned wise in their generation, while the few who looked forward to the future glories, were accounted by the bustlers, or heapers, to be either fools or mad.

Most of these pilgrims went on in adorning their dwellings, adding to their heaps, grasping "the things below" as if they would never let them go [their houses being built on sand; see Matt. 7:26—Ed.], shutting their eyes instead of using their telescope, and neglecting their title-deed [gift of life in Christ] as if it was the parchment of another man's estate, and not of their own, until, one after another, each felt his dwelling tumbling about his ears.

Oh, then what a busy, bustling, anxious, terrifying, distracting moment was that! What a deal of business was to be done, and what a strange time was this to do it in! Now to see the confusion and dismay, occasioned by having left everything to the last minute. First someone was sent for to make over the yellow heaps to another [gold], which the heaper now found would be of no use to himself in crossing the gulf—a transfer which ought to have been made while the dwelling was sound.

Then there was a consultation between two or three masons [spiritual physicians in her allegory—Ed.] at once, perhaps to try to patch up the walls, and strengthen the props, and stop the decay of the tumbling dwelling; but not until the masons were forced to declare it was past repairing—a truth they were rather too willing to keep back—did the tenant seriously think it was time to pack up, prepare, and be gone.

Then what sending for the 'wise men' who professed to explain the title-deed; and Oh, what remorse that they had neglected to examine it until their senses were too confused for so weighty a business! What reproaches, or what exhortations to others to look better after their own affairs than they had done! Even to the wisest of the inhabitants, the falling of their dwelling was a solemn thing—solemn, but not surprising; they had long been packing up and preparing; they praised their Lord's goodness that they had been allowed to stay so long; many acknowledged the mercy of their frequent warnings, and confessed that those very dilapidations which had made the house uncomfortable had been a blessing, as it had set them on diligent preparation for their future inheritance, had made them more earnest in examining their title to it, and had set them on such a frequent application to the telescope, that "the things above" had seemed every day to approach nearer and nearer, and "the things below" to recede and vanish in proportion. These desired not to be "unclothed, but to be clothed with their heavenly dwelling;" for they knew if the earthly tent they lived in was destroyed, they had a building from God, an eternal house in heaven, not built by human hands.

"These all died in faith, not having received the promises, but having seen them afar off, and were persuaded of them, and embraced them, and confessed that they were strangers and pilgrims on the earth." Hebrews 11:13

"Dearly beloved, I beseech you as strangers and pilgrims, abstain from fleshly lusts, which war against the soul." 1 Peter 2:11

Worth Thinking About

The Internet has made it more possible than ever to see the message of the stars about the glory of God's handiwork. Why not take some time this week to search the Internet for a phrase taken from Psalm 19? The search will not only turn up items on the verse itself in many different translations, but will also bring up many astonishing photographs of the universe available from telescopes around the world and the Hubble telescope still circling in outer space.

God's Witness in the Stars

The heavens declare the glory of God;

And the firmament shows His handiwork.

Day unto day utters speech,

And night unto night reveals knowledge.

There is no speech nor language

Where their voice is not heard.

Their line has gone out through all the earth,

And their words to the end of the world.

—Psalm 19:1-4

 Prayer

DEAR FATHER, THERE IS A MESSAGE OF YOUR GLORY EVERY NIGHT IN THE SKY. HELP ME TO LOOK UP AND PONDER THE WONDER OF YOUR CREATION. AMEN.

How Can I Explain Heaven to My Children?

Billy Graham

Evangelist to more people than anyone else in history—through radio, television and film appearances—Dr. Billy Graham has traveled the globe calling on people to repent and accept Christ as Savior. Now "retired" and in his 90s, he is probably the world's most famous evangelical Christian. In his book *Facing Death: And the Life After*, published by W Publishing group in 1987, Dr. Graham talks about how he would handle a child's questions about heaven.

In *Children's Letters to God*, a little boy wrote, "Dear God, What is it like when a person dies? Nobody will tell me. I just want to know, I don't want to do it. Your friend, Mike."

If I could answer Mike, I would first sit down with my arms around him and say, "Mike, everything must die sometime. When someone is dead, the body they have lived in stops breathing and moving, and seeing, and hearing. The person who had that body doesn't hurt or worry any longer. That is his earthly body. But we also have a spirit, Mike, and when we ask Jesus to come into our hearts, we will have a spiritual body from heaven. You see, son, God tells us that we will have new bodies that are strong and healthy, that are supernatural, spiritual bodies."

LOSING A LOVED ONE

Mike, and all the children like him, needs simple, honest answers and lots of love. If Mike should have someone he loved die, he needs to be able to express himself without being judged for his actions. He may show indifference or anger. He may revert to baby habits.

One friend told me about his eleven-year-old son, who developed a clinging attitude after the death of his big brother. The boy would cry if his parents wanted to go out for the evening. He wouldn't go anywhere without Mom or Dad. He left for a weekend with the Boy Scouts and became sick to his stomach before the troop reached their campsite. Fortunately, an understanding counselor brought him home without forcing him to stay. . . .

Children feel the need to talk about the death of a loved one, just as adults do. Stephen was eleven when his father died. He said in an interview, "I stayed home from school for two weeks and when I went back I wasn't crying anymore. My friends said, 'It doesn't seem like you're very sad your father died. It doesn't seem like you miss him.' I did feel sad, but I just didn't want to cry in front of them, you know. One kid even said, 'You must be glad your father died because you're not crying.' That remark really got me so upset that I told my mom about it when I got home. She said it was because when they saw me, it made them all think how sad they would be if their fathers died and they didn't realize I had done all my crying at home."

Stephen continued, "I don't know if I'll ever see my father again. No one really knows about heaven because they haven't been dead yet. But I think part of my father is still with me. His body isn't, but his spirit is. If he's anywhere, I guess he's in heaven with my grandfather. At night I usually pray to God and say, 'Please help Dad and Grandpop to have a fun time up there.'"

I would like to tell all the Stephens out there that, yes, there really is a heaven. Jesus came from there and He died and has gone back to prepare a place for us.

Worth Thinking About

How did you learn about heaven? Was it in church or at home? Considering Jesus' concern for children, how would you introduce the subject of death to them? Did you ever had someone explain about death to you when you were young? Did you feel comforted afterward or only more alarmed and confused and angry?

OH, HOW I LOVE JESUS

There is a Name I love to hear,

I love to sing its worth;

It sounds like music in my ear,

The sweetest Name on earth.

Oh, how I love Jesus,

Oh, how I love Jesus,

Oh, how I love Jesus,

Because he first loved me . . . !

It tells me what my Father hath

In store for every day,

And though I tread a darksome path,

Yields sunshine all the way.

—Frederick Whitfield

Prayer

DEAR FATHER, MAY YOU GIVE US THE WORDS TO SPEAK WHEN WE ANSWER CHILDREN'S QUESTIONS ABOUT HEAVEN AND WHERE THEIR DEAD LOVED ONES HAVE GONE. HELP US TO BE SENSITIVE TO THEIR LEVEL OF UNDERSTANDING AND TO MAKE OURSELVES CLEAR FOR THEIR SAKES. AMEN.

How Are the Different Meanings for the Word "Heaven" Explained in the Bible?

Herbert Lockyer (1886-1984)

Herbert Lockyer is best known for his famous series *All the Men of the Bible, All the Women of the Bible,* etc. . . . which came out over the course of his life in twenty-one volumes. Born in London, he ministered in the United Kingdom for twenty-five years before coming to America to have a long and extensive ministry here. This excerpt from *The Gospel of the Life Beyond* was published by Fleming Revell in 1967 and provides a guideline for how the word *heaven* is used in Scripture. Lockyer believed the Bible presented a unified view of heaven, in its various aspects, Genesis through to the Book of Revelation.

Sir John Suckling (1609 to1642) wrote:

'Tis expectation makes a blessing dear;
Heaven were not Heaven, if we knew what it were.

While we do not know all we would like to regarding the whereabouts of Heaven and all it represents, enough has been revealed to feed our expectation. . . .

If we accept the doctrine of a future life as taught by Christ, Prophets and Apostles, then we must have some sphere in which to live such a life. Certain, as He was, of the reality of

Heaven, seeing He had lived there before He was born a child in Bethlehem, Christ never told His disciples where it was located. When He addressed them in the upper chamber, He did not give them an elaborate description of the position in which Heaven lay, but simply comforted their hearts by assuring them that there was such a place in His Father's home, and that He was specially going away to prepare it for them. . . .

An examination of the terms used in connection with Heaven may prove profitable at this point. Cosmologically, it was one of the two great divisions of the universe. "In the beginning God created the heaven and the earth" (Gen. 1:1; Ezek. 32:7-8). We have heaven, earth, and water under the earth (Ex. 20:4). In the visible heavens there are the stars and planets (Gen. 1:14-17). Heaven and Earth, as terms, exclude one another, but together constitute the universe of God (Gen. 2:1; Matt. 5:18; 1 Cor. 8:5). God, as the Most High, is "possessor of heaven and earth" (Gen. 14:19-22), and Jesus recognized His Father as "Lord of heaven and earth" (Matt. 11:25). The original simple distribution of all things in the universe under the phrase "heaven and earth" is sometimes expanded as, for instance, by John in his description, "heaven and the earth and the sea and the fountains of water" (Rev. 14:7). The vast expanse above and around our earth is phenomenally like one of the ancient mirrors made of firm molten polished metal. "Spread out . . . strong . . . as a molten looking glass" (Gen. 1:16; Job 37:18; Isa. 44:24), *Heaven* is used of the surrounding air wherein "the fowls of heaven fly" (Gen. 1:20, 26). From it, rain and hail fall (Deut. 11:11). "I will make your heaven as iron," that is "your sky hard yielding not rain" (Lev. 26:19). "The four corners of heaven" and "the circuit of heaven" (Job 22:14; Jer. 49:36) are phrases referring to the atmospheric heaven. . . .

The Firmament, with its stars and planets. "When I consider the Heavens . . . the moon, and the stars" (Ps. 8:3).

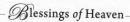

The Aerial Heaven, where the birds fly, the winds blow, and the showers are formed. "Windows of heaven were opened" (Gen. 7:11), represents the atmosphere on which the clouds float and out of which rain comes, Malachi uses the same phrase, figuratively, to describe the revival blessings from the Lord (3:10). Closed heavens indicate drought, both materially and spiritually (James 5:17, 18; Ps. 66:18).

The phrase, "The heaven of heavens," is a Hebraism for "the highest heaven" (Deut. 10:14; Ps. 68:33; 148:4), and represents the heavens par excellence, and agrees with the fuller phrase, "the heaven and the heaven of heavens," which was the sphere Paul reached when he was caught up to after passing through the first heaven—the air; [and] second heaven—the sky of the stars (2 Cor. 12:2). Christ was "made higher than the heavens" and passed through the heavens, namely, the aerial heaven and the starry heaven (Eph. 4:10; Heb. 4:14; 7:26). He passed through the outer veils and then through the veil into the holy of holies, or the immediate presence of God. "The height of heaven" (1 Kings 8:27) whose top can be reached. Here we have an unusual hyperbole expressing a great height (Deut. 1:28; 9:1). As a term, *Heavens* is used to describe the powerful providence of God (Dan. 4:26)—that which is good and honorable (Luke 15:18)—political or ecclesiastical government (Isa. 13:13; Haggai 2:6, 21). The aerial and starry heavens are to pass away and burn up (2 Peter 3:7, 10), and in their place will appear the new heavens and earth. *Heaven,* God's abode, is stable and permanent.

Worth Thinking About

Every time we pray the Lord's Prayer, or the model prayer Jesus taught his disciples, we ask that his will "be done on earth, as it is in heaven." Do you feel you now have a clearer view of what you have been asking for or does Dr. Lockyer's explanation of the different uses of the word heaven still leave you with questions? When does mere curiosity end and real need to know begin?

I AM SO GLAD THAT MY FATHER IN HEAVEN

I am so glad that my Father in heaven
Tells of His love in the Book He has given;
Wonderful things in the Bible I see—
This is the dearest, that Jesus loves me. . . .
O if there's only one song I can sing,
When in His beauty I see the great King,
This shall my song in eternity be:
"Oh, what a wonder that Jesus loves me!"

—P. P. Bliss

Prayer

DEAR FATHER, HELP YOUR CHILDREN TO WORK FOR THE DAY WHEN HEAVEN AND EARTH ARE ONE IN LOVING YOU. MAY OUR INTEREST IN HEAVEN BE MORE THAN JUST MERE CURIOSITY. AMEN.

HAVE YOU EVER THOUGHT OF DEATH AS A GIFT?

Erwin Lutzer

"The last enemy to be destroyed is death," says a famous Scripture passage from First Corinthians 15:26 (NIV), and yet pastor Erwin Lutzer of Moody Church in Chicago gives us a different perspective by reminding us that we have been "given" death in a way that makes it our "possession" (see 1 Cor. 3:21-23). What sort of change in perspective does it give you to think of death, not as a roadblock to life, but as a doorway to heaven? Dr. Lutzer is a prominent radio broadcaster heard around the world, and this selection comes from his book *One Minute after You Die,* from Moody Publishers in 2007.

❧

After Adam and Eve sinned, they died spiritually as well as physically. Sending them out of the garden, far from being an act of cruelty, was actually proof of God's kindness. We read, "'he might stretch out his hand, and take also from the tree of life, and eat, and live forever'—therefore the Lord God sent him out from the garden of Eden, to cultivate the ground from which he was taken" (Genesis 3:22-23).

If Adam and Eve had eaten of the other special tree of the garden—the Tree of Life—they would have been immortalized in their sinful condition. They never would have qualified for the heaven that God wanted them to enjoy. Imagine living forever as sinners, with no possibility of redemption and permanent transformation. Although they would never have to face the finality of death, they would have been condemned to a pitiful existence.

Thus God prevented Adam and Eve from eternal sinfulness by giving them the gift of death, the ability to exit this life and arrive safely in the wondrous life to come. Death, though it would appear to be man's greatest enemy, would in the end, prove to be his greatest friend. Only through death can we go to God (unless, of course, we are still living when Christ returns).

That is why Paul classified death as one of the possessions of the Christian. "All things belong to you, whether Paul or Apollos or Cephas or the world or life or death or things present or things to come; all things belong to you, and you belong to Christ; and Christ belongs to God" (1 Corinthians 3:21-23). We should not be surprised that death is listed as one of the gifts that belongs to us. Only death can give us the gift of eternity. . . .

Think of how powerless death actually is! Rather than rid us of our wealth, it introduces us to "riches eternal." In exchange for poor health, death gives us a right to the Tree of Life that is for "the healing of the nations" (Revelation 22:2). Death might temporarily take our friends from us, but only to introduce us to that land in which there are no good-byes.

That is why Christ could say, "Do not fear those who kill the body but are unable to kill the soul; but rather fear Him who is able to destroy both soul and body in hell" (Matthew 10:28). The body might temporarily be the possession of cancer or evil men, but these enemies cannot prevent the soul from going to God. When the executioners have done their worst, God will be shown to have done His best.

Worth Thinking About

So, death is an "enemy," but it is also the door through which we must go to inherit life eternal and all the joys of heaven. Death came through sin, Scripture says, but God absolutely manages death. How does this make a difference in our perspective? Is death an accident that happens to us or is it the thing God controls to his glory, even though we cannot always see how that is. What part does faith play in facing death? Why is it so hard to accept the death of a young child? God promises to bring good out of the travail and sorrow, yet some events still challenge us all the same.

HIS BANNER OVER US IS LOVE

His banner over us is love, our sword the Word of God;
We tread the road the saints above with shouts of triumph trod.
By faith they, like a whirlwind's breath swept on o'er every field;
The faith by which they conquered Death is still our shining shield.

Faith is the victory! Faith is the victory!

Oh, glorious victory that overcomes the world.

—John H. Yates

Prayer

DEAR FATHER, GRANT US DETERMINATION TO FOLLOW YOU IN LIFE AND THANK YOU THAT OUR DEATH WILL BE A GLORIOUS ENTRANCE INTO THE JOYS OF HEAVEN. HELP US TO TRUST YOUR TIMING FOR EVENTS THAT ARE OUT OF OUR CONTROL. AMEN.

WILL MY PET GO TO HEAVEN?

Randy Alcorn

Since founding Eternal Perspectives Ministry in 1990, former pastor Randy Alcorn has published over forty books on topics related to eternity and heaven. His books have sold some seven million copies. It isn't just children who have wondered about whether their pets will be in heaven. Many adults have loved their animals and wondered the same thing. This answer to whether or not animals will be in heaven comes from Alcorn's book *Heaven,* published by Tyndale House in 2004.

Christ proclaims from his throne on the New Earth: "Behold, I am making all things new" (Revelation 21:5, ESV). It's not just people who will be renewed but also the earth and "all things" in it. Do "all things" include animals? Yes. . . .

HOW CLOSELY ARE ANIMALS TIED TO OUR RESURRECTION?

Did Christ die for animals? Certainly not in the way he died for mankind. People are made in God's image, animals aren't. People sinned, animals didn't. Because animals didn't sin, they don't need a redeemer in the same way.

But in another sense, Christ died for animals indirectly because his death for humanity purchased redemption for what was brought down by humanity's sin, including animals. Romans 8 is explicit on this point: "The creation itself will be liberated from its bondage to decay and brought into the glorious freedom of the children of God. . . . The whole creation has been groaning as in the pains of childbirth. . . . We wait eagerly for . . . the redemption of our bodies" (Romans 8:21-23). On the New Earth, after mankind's resurrection, animals who once suffered will join God's children in glorious freedom from death and decay. . . .

As goes mankind, so go the animals. If we take to its logical conclusions the parallel Paul makes between humans' and animals' groaning, then at least some of those animals who suffered on the old Earth must be made whole on the New Earth.

It's not some abstract "animalkind" that cries out. The creatures that groan and cry out for their resurrection are specific suffering people and specific animals. They cry out for their deliverance, not another's. I believe this suggests that God may remake certain animals that lived on the old Earth. . . .

This fits the words anticipating Christ's coming: "And all flesh will see the salvation of God" (Luke 3:6, NASB). The Greek world translated "flesh" is *sarx*. Some Bible versions translate this as "all people" or "all mankind," but the word is more inclusive. "All flesh" includes animals. They too will behold and benefit from Christ's redemptive work.

Psalm 104 demonstrates God's intimate involvement with the lives of his animals and his purposes for them. The psalm speaks of birds, cattle, wild donkeys, rock badgers, and lions, saying "the earth is full of your creatures" (v. 24). It speaks of "the sea, vast and spacious, teeming with creatures beyond number—living things both large and small" (v. 25). It says, "These all look to you" (v. 27). Then the psalm writer adds, "When you take away their breath, they die and return to the dust" (v. 29). But then we're told something amazing: "When you send your Spirit, they are created, and you renew the face of the earth" (v. 30). The "they" seems to refer to the animals who've died and returned to the dust. What does God mean that he sends his Spirit and creates them? It appears that he's talking about re-creating animals after they've died. Why? To "renew the face of the earth." The same "they" who die are the "they" who are created or re-created as part of the earth's renewal (Matthew 19:28).

Worth Thinking About

One of the first tasks given to Adam was to name the animals. Why would God think it important for the animals to be named? What other biblical passages can you think of that mention the importance of animals? (Read the story that Nathan the prophet told King David, 2 Samuel 12:1-4.)

THE GOOD SHEPHERD

I am the good shepherd. The good shepherd gives His life for the sheep. But he who is a hireling and not the shepherd, one who does not own the sheep, sees the wolf coming and leaves the sheep and flees; and the wolf catches them and scatters them. The hireling flees because he is a hireling and does not care about the sheep. I am the good shepherd; and I know My sheep, and am known by my own. As the Father knows Me, even so I know the Father; and I lay down My life for the sheep. And other sheep I have which are not of this fold; them also I must bring, and they will hear My voice; and there will be one flock and one shepherd. —John 10:11-14

Prayer

DEAR FATHER, THANK YOU FOR THE GIFT OF ANIMALS WHOM WE CAN LOVE AND CARE FOR. HELP US TO SHOW YOUR KINDNESS TO THEM AND TO LIVE UP TO OUR RESPONSIBILITY WITH REGARD TO YOUR MATERIAL AS WELL AS YOUR SPIRITUAL GIFTS. EVEN THIS FALLEN WORLD REVEALS YOUR POWER AND GLORY. HELP US TO CARE ABOUT ALL YOUR CREATION AND BE GOOD STEWARDS OF IT. AMEN.

What Taste of Heaven Now Hints of the Life to Come?

Charles H. Spurgeon

Founder of what was probably the largest protestant church of his day, Charles Haddon Spurgeon preached for many years at the Metropolitan Tabernacle in London. Seating in this great edifice was for several thousand people and Spurgeon spoke without the benefit of a microphone. His published sermons, still in print, run to almost sixty large volumes. This excerpt is from the sermon "Creation's Groans and Saints' Sighs" and was preached in 1868.

—◦◦◦—

If we have the "first-fruits of the Spirit," what will the full harvest be like?

We know that the whole creation groaneth and travaileth in pain together until now. And not only they, but ourselves also, which have the first-fruits of the Spirit, even we ourselves groan within ourselves, waiting for the adoption, to wit, the redemption of our body.—Romans 8:22-23.

Creation glows with a thousand beauties, even in its present fallen condition; yet clearly enough it is not as when it came from the Maker's hand—the slime of the serpent is on it all—this is not the world which God pronounced to be "very good." We hear of tornadoes, of earthquakes, of tempests, of volcanoes, of avalanches, and of the sea which devours its thousands: there is sorrow on the sea, and there is misery on the land; and into the highest palaces as well as the poorest cottages, death, the insatiable, is shooting his arrows, while his quiver is still full to bursting with future woes. It is a sad, sad world. The apostle tells us that not only is there a groan from creation, but this is shared in by God's people. . . .

We were once an undistinguished part of the creation, subject to the same curse as the rest of the world, "heirs of wrath, even as others." [Eph. 2:3] But distinguishing grace has made a difference where no difference naturally was; we are now no longer treated as criminals condemned, but as children and heirs of God. We have received a divine life, by which we are made partakers of the divine nature, having "escaped the corruption which is in the world through lust." [2 Pet. 1:4] The Spirit of God has come to us so that our "bodies are the temples of the Holy Ghost." [1 Cor. 6:19] God dwells in us, and we are one with Christ. We have at this present moment in us certain priceless things which distinguish us as believers in Christ from all the rest of God's creatures. *"We have,"* says the text, not "we hope and trust sometimes we have," nor yet "possibly we may have," but "we have, we know we have, we are sure we have."

Believing in Jesus, we speak confidently, we have unspeakable blessings given to us by the Father of spirits. Not we *shall have,* but *we have.* True, many things are yet in the future, but even at this present moment, we have obtained an inheritance; we have already in our possession a heritage divine which is the beginning of our eternal portion. This is called "the firstfruits of the Spirit," by which I understand the first works of the Spirit in our souls.

Brethren, we have repentance, that gem of the first water. We have faith, that priceless, precious jewel. We have hope, which sparkles, a hope most sure and steadfast. We have love, which sweetens all the rest. We have that work of the Spirit within our souls which always comes before admittance into glory. We are already made "new creatures in Christ Jesus," by the effectual working of the mighty lower of God the Holy Ghost. This is called the first-fruit because *it comes first.* As the wave-sheaf was the first of the harvest, so the spiritual life which we have, and all the graces which adorn that life, are the first gifts, the first operations of the Spirit of God in our souls. . . .

It is called "first-fruits," again, because *the first-fruits were always the pledge of the harvest.* As soon as the Israelite had plucked the first handful of ripe ears, they were to him so many proofs that the harvest was already come. He looked forward with glad anticipation to the time when the wagon should creak beneath the sheaves, and when the harvest home should be shouted at the door of the barn. So, brethren, when God gives us "Faith, hope, charity—these three," when he gives us "whatsoever things are pure, lovely, and of good report," as the work of the Holy Spirit, these are to us the prognostics of the coming glory. If you have the Spirit of God in your soul, you may rejoice over it as the pledge and token of the fullness of bliss and perfection "which God hath prepared for them that love him. . . ." [1 Cor. 2:9]

Brothers, the work of the Spirit is called "first-fruits," because *the first-fruits were not the harvest.* No Jew was ever content with the first-fruits. He was content with them for what they were, but the first-fruits enlarged his desires for the harvest. If he had taken the first-fruits home, and said, "I have all I want," and had rested satisfied month after month, he would have given proof of madness, for the first-fruit does but whet the appetite—does but stir up the desire it never was meant to satisfy. So, when we get the first works of the Spirit of God, we are not to say, "I have attained, I am already perfect, there is nothing further for me to do, or to desire." Nay, my brothers, all that the most advanced of God's people know as yet, should but excite in them an insatiable thirst after more. . . .

[Here is an example of the expectations of a rescued traveler—Ed.] He has been charitably received, he has been warmed at the fire, he has received abundant provision, he is warmly clothed. There is no fear of tempest, that grand old hospice has outstood many a thundering storm. The [traveler] is perfectly safe, and quite content, so far as that goes, and exceedingly grateful to think that he has been rescued; but yet I hear him groan because he has a wife and children down in yonder plain, and the snow is lying too deep for traveling, and the wind is howling, and the blinding snow flakes are falling so thickly that he cannot pursue his journey. Ask him whether he is happy and content. He says, "Yes, I am happy and grateful. I have been saved from the snow. I do not wish for anything more than I have here, I am perfectly satisfied, so far as this goes, but I long to look upon my household, and to be once more in my own sweet home, and until I reach it, I shall not cease to groan. . . ."

Such is the groan of the believer, who, though rescued and brought into the hospice of divine mercy, is longing to see his Father's face without a veil between, and to be united with the happy family on the other side of the Jordan, where they rejoice for evermore.

Worth Thinking About

Paul said he struggled both with a desire to depart and be with Christ or yet remain because he had service still to do. Do you think that some of his feelings might have come from his experience of having gone to the "third heaven"? [2 Cor. 12:2] Do you think Lazarus wanted to come back into this life from the dead? What first-fruits of heaven have you tasted?

THE LAST MILE OF THE WAY

Here the dearest of ties we must sever,
tears of sorrow are seen every day;

But no sickness, no sighing forever when we've gone
the last mile of the way.

When I've gone the last mile of the way,
I will rest at the close of the day.

And I know there are joys that await me
when I've gone the last mile of the way.

—Johnson Oatman

Prayer

DEAR FATHER, WE AWAIT WITH IMPATIENCE THE GREAT LIBERTY WE WILL EXPERIENCE AT THE REDEMPTION OF OUR BODY WHEN THE IMPERFECT WILL PUT ON THE PERFECT IN THE KINGDOM OF GOD. YET MAY WE BE RESPONSIBLE FOR OUR PART IN OUR OWN TRANSFORMATION NOW BY DOING WHAT YOU COMMAND AND SERVING OTHERS AS WE WOULD OURSELVES. AMEN.

ARE THE NEW HEAVEN AND THE NEW EARTH MENTIONED IN PLACES OTHER THAN THE BOOK OF REVELATION?

Dr. Dale Moody (1915–1991)

Of course, the new heaven and the new earth are specifically mentioned in Scripture in Revelation chapter 21, but some theologians have felt that many references to God's eternal kingdom can be found throughout the whole of Scripture. Here are Dr. Moody's observations from his classic book *The Hope of Glory*. By comparing Scripture with Scripture we can have greater light on the subject. After all, it is the whole counsel of God we want, not just proof texts, and the Bible is full of the hope of heaven and the nature of heaven from one end to the other.

"Once again, in a little while, I will shake the heavens and the earth and the sea and the dry land; and I will shake all nations, so that the treasures of all nations shall come in, and I will fill this house with splendor, says the Lord of hosts. The silver is mine, and the gold is mine, says the Lord of hosts. The latter splendor of this house shall be greater than the former, says the Lord of hosts; and in this place I will give prosperity, says the Lord of hosts" (Hag. 2:6-9). Jerusalem is "this place" where the glory and splendor of God will be made known—the eschatological Jerusalem, the place of endless *shalom* (prosperity, peace).

To Zechariah the promise is made (Zech. 8:3): "I will return to Zion, and will dwell in the midst of Jerusalem, and Jerusalem shall be called the faithful city, and the mountain of the Lord of hosts, the holy mountain" (cf. 2:10).

God dwells in heaven, but He descends to dwell with His people. One of the most notable examples of "the paradox of grace" in the Old Testament, which expresses God's transcendence and immanence, remoteness and nearness, is the oracle on the divine dwelling place in Isaiah 57:15:

> For thus says the high and lofty One
> who inhabits eternity, whose name is Holy:
> "I dwell in the high and holy place,
> and also with him who is of contrite and humble spirit,
> to revive the spirit of the humble,
> and to revive the heart of the contrite."

No other call to worship and reverence binds God to His people more closely and brings more hope that He will ultimately dwell with His people for ever. . . .

The full splendor of this dawning glory is focused on the eschatological Jerusalem, of which the earthly one is but a frail symbol. The vision is real and the voice is sure in Isaiah 65:17f.:

> "For behold, I create new heavens
> and a new earth;
> and the former things shall not be remembered
> or come into mind.
> But be glad and rejoice for ever
> in that which I create;
> for behold, I create Jerusalem a rejoicing,
> and her people a joy."

Such visions are of glory that only God can give from His throne in heaven to His children on His footstool on earth below (66:1).

As the earthly symbol of God's abode with His people, Jerusalem stirred feelings expressed in what has been called "Songs of Zion" (Ps. 38, 84, 87, 122, 126), sung by pilgrims as they made the journey to the sacred festivals with hopes of an ideal future and final glory. Psalm 48 speaks of Jerusalem as "the city of our God" (vv. 1, 8). There is God's "dwelling" and "house" (Ps. 84:1, 4; 122:1, 9). In the spirit of these pilgrims' Psalms, Isaac Watts sang:

> The hill of Zion yields
> A thousand sacred sweets
> Before we reach the heavenly fields,
> Or walk the golden streets.

All this is symbolism, to be sure, but it symbolizes an ultimate reality that is awesome and sublime, a mystery before which men can only wonder and worship.

---

*W*orth Thinking About

The traditional view of the church down through the centuries is that there is an essential unity to Scripture: after all, the Holy Bible begins with a beginning and definitely ends with an ending, and a complete story of redemption is told in between. But with the rise of the concept that each passage of Scripture should be interpreted in the context in which it was originally given, the belief in the general unity of Scripture has been less emphasized. How do you feel? Do

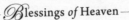

Old Testament references foreshadow New Testament endings? Does Scripture fit together for you as one whole?

WHAT GLORY GILDS THE SACRED PAGE

What glory gilds the sacred page majestic like the sun;

It gives a light to every age; it gives but borrows none.

The hand that gave it still supplies the gracious light and heat;

His truths upon the nations rise: they rise, but never set.

—William Cowper

Prayer

DEAR FATHER, HELP ME TO SEE THE STORY OF YOUR REDEMPTION AND TO LOVE IT ON EVERY SACRED PAGE OF YOUR WORD. HELP ME TO RETURN TO YOUR WORD FOR EACH CHOICE I MAKE AND SIMPLY TO REST IN YOUR PRESENCE. AMEN.

Will Heaven Be Big Enough to Hold Everyone?

John MacArthur

John MacArthur is a busy man. Founder of The Master's Seminary, Grace to You—an international radio program—and The Master's College, he still serves as pastor-teacher at Grace Community Church in Sun Valley, California. His books have sold in the millions of copies. Dr. MacArthur interprets the Bible literally and believes there is a solid answer to the size of heaven. His comments come from *The MacArthur New Testament Commentary: Revelation 12-22* published by Moody Press in 2000.

⧉

The one who spoke with me had a gold measuring rod to measure the city, and its gates and its wall. The city is laid out as a square, and its length is as great as the width; and he measured the city with the rod, fifteen hundred miles; its length and width and height are equal. And he measured its wall, seventy-two yards, according to human measurements, which are also angelic measurements. The material of the wall was jasper; and the city was pure gold, like clear glass. The foundation stones of the city wall were adorned with every kind of precious stone. The first foundation stone was jasper; the second sapphire; the third, chalcedony; the fourth, emerald; the fifth, sardonyx; the sixth, sardius; the seventh, chrysolite; the eighth beryl;

the ninth, topaz; the tenth, chrysoprase; the eleventh, jacinth; the twelfth, amethyst. And the twelve gates were twelve pearls; each one of the gates was a single pearl. (Rev. 21:15-21a)

Human language is inadequate to fully describe the unimaginable magnificence of the believer's indescribable eternal home. Unwilling to take the language of Scripture at face value, many seek for some hidden meaning behind John's description. But if the words do not mean what they say, who has the authority to say what they do mean? Abandoning the literal meaning of the text leads only to baseless, groundless, futile speculation. The truth about the heavenly city is more than is described, but not less and not different from what is described. It is a material creation, yet so unique as to be unimaginable to us. The words of John provide all the detail we have been given by God to excite our hope.

That the city "had a great high wall" indicates that it is not an amorphous, nebulous, floating place. It has specific dimensions; it has limits; it can be entered and left through its "twelve gates." At those "gates twelve angels" were stationed, to attend to God's glory and to serve His people (cf. Heb. 1:14). The "gates" had "names . . . written on them, which are the names of the twelve tribes of the sons of Israel" celebrating for all eternity God's covenant relationship with Israel, the people of the promises, the covenants, the Scriptures, and the Messiah. They were arranged symmetrically; "there were three gates on the east and three gates on the north and three gates on the south and three gates on the west." That arrangement is reminiscent of the way the twelve tribes camped around the tabernacle (Num. 2), and of the allotment of the tribal lands around the millennial temple (Ezek. 48).

The massive "wall of the city" was anchored by "twelve foundation stones, and on them were the twelve names of the twelve apostles of the Lamb." Those "stones" commemorate God's covenant relationship with the church, of which the apostles are the foundation (Eph. 2:20). At the top of each gate was the name of one of the tribes of Israel; at the bottom of each gate was the name of one of the apostles. Thus, the layout of the city's gates pictures God's favor on all His redeemed people, both those under the old covenant, and those under the new covenant.

Then a curious thing occurred. The angel "who spoke with" John "had a gold measuring rod to measure the city, and its gates and its wall." This interesting event is reminiscent of the measuring of the millennial temple (Ezek. 40:3ff.) and the measuring of the Tribulation temple (11:1). The significance of all three measurements is that they mark out what belongs to God.

The results of the angel's measuring revealed that "the city is laid out as a square, and its length is as great as the width; and he measured the city with the rod, fifteen hundred miles" (lit. "12,000 *stadia*"; a *stadion* was about 607 feet. Thus, the city walls are about 1,380 miles in each direction); "its length and width and height are equal." Some commentators have suggested that the city is in the shape of a pyramid. It is best seen as a cube; however, as Henry M. Morris [author and creationist—Ed.] points out:

> Such an interpretation is quite forced, however, the language of the passage being much more naturally understood to mean a cube, with the length and breadth and height all the same. . . .

> The cube . . . was the shape specified by God for the holy place . . . in Solomon's temple (1 Kings 6:20), where God was to "dwell" between the cherubim. Both the language and the symbology thus favor the

cubical, rather than the pyramidal, shape (*The Revelation Record* [Wheaton, Ill.: Tyndale, 1983], 450)

Morris also points out that a cube-shaped city is well-suited for the existence of glorified beings:

> It should also be remembered that the new bodies of the resurrected saints will be like those of angels, no longer limited by gravitational or electromagnetic forces as at present. Thus it will be easy for the inhabitants to travel vertically as horizontally, in the new Jerusalem. Consequently, the "streets" of the city (verse 21) may well include vertical passageways as well as horizontal avenues, and the "blocks" could be real cubical blocks, instead of square areas between streets as in a present-day earthly city. (*The Revelation Record, 451*)

Based on certain assumptions about the design of the city and the number of the redeemed who will live in it, Morris calculates that each person's "cube" would be approximately seventy-five acres on each side (*The Revelation Record*, 451). . . . Obviously, God will design the new Jerusalem with plenty of room for all the redeemed (cf. John 14:2-3).

Worth Thinking About

Such a city as here described by MacArthur may have room for several billion people, according to Catholic theologian Peter Kreeft. A literal cube over 1,000 miles long on each side would have plenty of room for those whose names are written in "the Lamb's Book of Life" (Rev. 21:27). Have you ever considered the size of the heavenly city? What can be the significance of its vastness in comparison

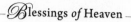

with earthly cities? Verse 9 of Revelation 7 suggests there will be a great multitude in heaven "which no one could number." There will be plenty of room for those who come to him by faith.

Oh, Lord, Thou Hast Ascended

Sing unto God, you nations, you kingdoms of the earth;
Sing unto God, all people, and praise His matchless worth.
He rides in royal triumph upon the heavens abroad;
He speaks, the mountains tremble before the voice of God.

—Lowell Mason

rayer

Dear Father, may countless billions believe in you; for you are not willing that any should perish but that all should come to repentance (see 2 Pet. 3:9). May we, your servants, spread the news of your salvation everywhere. Amen.

Can the Promise of Heaven Be Used As an Evangelistic Tool?

Catherine of Genoa (1447–1550)

Winning people to Christ takes more forms than can be mentioned here. But there are some earnest Christians who would scare you in, some who would woo you in, and some who would preach you in. Catherine of Genoa, a matron of a hospital affiliated with the Franciscans, was a wooer: she felt that God took account of our human frailties and directed that the rewards of heaven would be so great that we would *want* to go there rather than *have* to go there to get fire insurance from the dangers of hell. This insight is taken from *Devotional Classics: Selected Readings for Individuals and Groups*, edited by Richard Foster and James Bryan Smith, and was published by HarperCollins in 1993.

God's Clever Strategy

The selfishness that is within us, however, is so contrary to God that God cannot induce us to do his will except by a clever strategy: promising us greater things than what the world can give—even in this life—and promising a kind of consolation that the world does not know. God does this, I think, because he knows how much we are attached to pleasure. He knows that we are the kind who will not leave our one little toy unless we are offered four!

Vision of the Life to Come

If we could see what we will receive in the life to come (as a reward for what we have done here), we would cease to occupy ourselves with anything but the things of heaven. But God, who desires that we see by faith and who desires that we do not do good because of selfish motives, gives us this vision little by little, sufficient to the level of faith of which we are capable. In this manner, God leads up into a greater vision of that which is to come until faith is no longer needed.

On the other hand, if we were somehow informed that we were about to die, and that the life that awaits us will be miserable because of our sins, and that we would have to suffer eternally, I feel sure that we—for fear of it—would rather let ourselves be killed than commit one single sin! But God—as unwilling as he is that we avoid sin out of the motive of fear and therefore never lets us see it—will show it in part to souls who are clothed and occupied with him.

STEADFAST TRUST

May this be our prayer: "I do not want to turn my eyes from you, O God. There I want them to stay and not to move no matter what happens to me, within or without." For those who trust in God need not worry about themselves. As I think about you, my spiritual children, I see that God's pure love is attentive to all of your needs. It is because of this tender love that I need not ask anything of God for you. All I need to do is lift you up before his face.

---

*W*orth Thinking About

There are many ways in which people are weaned away from the world and brought to their Savior. How were you won to Christ? Do you think that people can be so attracted by the joys of heaven that they would want to go? *The Shorter Catechism of the Westminster*

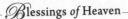
Standards asks: "What is the chief end of man?" And the answer is given: "Man's chief end is to glorify God, and to enjoy Him for ever." Has anybody ever caught you enjoying God?

REJOICE, YE PURE IN HEART

Rejoice, ye pure in heart, rejoice, give thanks and sing;

Your festal banner wave on high—the cross of Christ your King;

Rejoice, rejoice, rejoice, give thanks and sing.

With all the angel choirs, with all the saints on earth,

Pour out the strains of joy and bliss, true rapture, noblest mirth.

Rejoice, rejoice, rejoice, give thanks and sing.

—Edward H. Plumptre

Prayer

DEAR FATHER, AS JOY IS ONE OF THE FRUITS OF YOUR SPIRIT, HELP US TO LEARN WHAT IT IS TO ENJOY YOU FOREVER. LET US BE THE KIND OF PEOPLE WHO WOO OTHERS TO YOU BY THE POWER OF A POSITIVE AFFECTION. HELP US TO KNOW WHAT IT MEANS TO ENJOY GOD. AMEN.

WON'T WE BE JEALOUS IF OTHERS RECEIVE GREATER REWARDS IN HEAVEN THAN WE DO?

Jonathan Edwards (1703-1758)

Congregationalist minister Jonathan Edwards is known primarily for one sermon that many people find simply appalling, his "Sinners in the Hands of an Angry God." Once required reading in many high school English textbooks, it was held up as an example of the typical abuses of a religious fanatic, or so the secular texts would have it. It certainly cannot be denied that Edwards preached this sermon to a congregation made up of many members who, although they had taken the sacrament of baptism and some had taken communion, did not acknowledge a vital conversion experience then required for full membership. How this came about cannot be explained here, but it would have been a difficult situation for any minister whose congregation lived in what was called a "half-way covenant." However, a sermon more representative of Edwards at this crucial time in his ministry is "Heaven: A World of Love." Although this sermon certainly gives a different picture of Edwards, its primary value lies in drawing us to heaven through a presentation of the love practiced there entirely free of any coercion or fear.

❦

> Charity never faileth: but whether there be prophecies, they shall fail; whether there be tongues, they shall cease; whether there be knowledge, it shall vanish away (1 Cor. 13:8).

Christ loves all his saints in heaven. His love flows out to his whole church there, and to every individual member of it. And they all, with one heart and one soul, unite in love to their common Redeemer. Every heart is wedded to this holy and spiritual husband, and all rejoice in him, while the angels join them in their love. And the angels and saints all love each other. All the members of the glorious society of heaven are sincerely united. There is not a single secret or open enemy among them all. Not a heart is there that is not full of love, and not a solitary inhabitant that is not beloved by all the others. And as all are lovely, so all see each other's loveliness with full [acceptance] and delight. Every soul goes out in love to every other; and among all the blessed inhabitants, love is mutual, and full, and eternal. . . .

Of the principle of love in heaven. —And by this I mean, the love itself that fills and blesses the heavenly world, and which may be noticed both as to its nature and degree. And . . . in its nature, this love is altogether holy and divine. Most of the love that there is in this world is of an unhallowed nature. But the love that has place in heaven is not carnal but spiritual. It does not proceed from corrupt principles or selfish motives, nor is it directed to mean and vile purposes and ends. As opposed to all this, it is a pure flame, directed by holy motives, and aiming at no ends inconsistent with God's glory and the happiness of the universe. The saints in heaven love God for his own sake, and each other for God's sake, and for the sake of the relation that they have to him, and the image of God that is upon them. . . .

As to its degree.—And in degree it is perfect. The love that dwells in the heart of God is perfect, with an absolutely infinite and divine perfection. The love of angels and saints to God and Christ, is perfect in its kind, or with such a perfection as is proper to their nature. It is perfect with a sinless perfection, and perfect in that it is commensurate to the capacities of their nature. So it is said in the text, that "when that which is perfect is come, that which is in part shall be done away." Their love shall be without any remains of any contrary principle, having no pride or selfishness to interrupt it or hinder its exercises. Their hearts shall be full of love. That which was in the heart on earth as but a grain of mustard-seed, shall be as a great tree in heaven. The soul that in this world had only a little spark of divine love in it, in heaven shall be, as it were, turned into a bright and ardent flame, like the sun in its fullest brightness, when it has no spot upon it.

In heaven there shall be no remaining enmity, or distaste, or coldness, or deadness of heart towards God and Christ. Not the least remainder of any principle of envy shall exist to be exercised toward angels or other beings who are superior in glory; nor shall there be aught like contempt or slighting of those who are inferiors. Those that have a lower station in glory than others, suffer no diminution of their own happiness by seeing others above them in glory. On the contrary, all the members of that blessed society rejoice in each other's happiness, for the love of benevolence is perfect in them all. Every one has not only a sincere, but a perfect goodwill to every other. Sincere and strong love is greatly gratified and delighted in the prosperity of the beloved object; and if the love be perfect, the greater the prosperity of the beloved is, the more is the lover pleased and delighted; for the prosperity of the beloved is, as it were, the food of love, and therefore the greater that prosperity, the more richly is love feasted. . . .

There is undoubtedly an inconceivably pure, sweet, and fervent love between the saints in glory; and that love is in proportion to the perfection and amiableness of the objects beloved, and therefore it must necessarily cause delight in them when they see that the happiness and glory of others are in proportion to their amiableness, and so in proportion to their love to them. Those that are highest in glory, are those that are highest in holiness, and therefore are those that are most beloved by all the saints; for they most love those that are most holy, and so they will all rejoice in their being the most happy. And it will not be a grief to any of the saints to see those that are higher than themselves in holiness and likeness to God, more loved also than themselves, for all shall have as much love as they desire, and as great manifestations of love as they can bear; and so all shall be fully satisfied; and where there is perfect satisfaction, there can be no reason for envy. And there will be no temptation for any to envy those that are above them in glory, on account of the latter being lifted up with pride; for there will be no pride in heaven. We are not to conceive that those who are more holy and happy than others in heaven will be elated and lifted up in their spirit above others; for those who are above others in holiness, will be superior to them in humility. The saints that are highest in glory will be the lowest in humbleness of mind, for their superior humility is part of their superior holiness. . . .

And, besides, the inferior in glory will have no temptation to envy those that are higher than themselves, for those that are highest will not only be more loved by the lower for their higher holiness, but they will also have more of the spirit of love to others, and so will love those that are below them more than if their own capacity and elevation were less.

⋙⋘

Worth Thinking About

Many people are perfectly willing to take it on faith that there won't be envy in heaven, but when one considers the scriptural truth that there will be a difference in rewards, including who will sit closest to

Christ in glory (see Mark 10:35-37), one sees that the "stakes" of winning this "reward" will be higher than any other. Do you rejoice when others rejoice? Are you glad when someone achieves something above what you have done? This is truly putting the interest of others before your own. If you are able to rejoice now in someone else's achievement, you will be even more inclined to do so in heaven, which will be part of the glory of being there. To be delivered from selfishness is something to be strongly desired.

'TIS SO SWEET TO TRUST IN JESUS

Yes, 'tis sweet to trust in Jesus, just from sin and self to cease;

Just from Jesus simply taking life and rest, and joy and peace.

Jesus, Jesus, how I trust Him! How I've proved Him o'er and o'er!

Jesus, Jesus, precious Jesus! O for grace to trust Him more!

—Louisa M. R. Stead

Prayer

DEAR FATHER, THANK YOU FOR THE RELIEF OF LEAVING OUR MANY SINS BEHIND US WHEN WE GO TO BE WITH YOU. MAY WE EVER LIVE REPENTANT LIVES AND SEEK TO CONFESS OUR SINS AND TO MAKE AMENDS WHEN WE DO WRONG. HELP US TO VALUE A RIGHT RELATIONSHIP WITH YOU AND WITH OTHERS. AMEN.

Can an Illness Draw Us Closer to Heaven?

Lady Juliana of Norwich (ca. 1342 –1416)

There is no book in the world quite like *Revelations of Divine Love.* Some scholars believe it to be the first book in English to be written by a woman, and a largely unknown woman at that. Juliana (often times called Julian because that was the name of the church with which this anchorite—cloistered person— was associated) apparently lived from approximately 1342 to 1416. It is unlikely that she was a nun, but, in any case, she fell severely ill at about age thirty and nearly died. Out of her illness she received a number of visions of Jesus. Her shorter version of these experiences were apparently written down by herself and then later extended into a longer version, which is the version most often now published. Her reassuring conclusion from her experiences with Christ during her sickness is often quoted: "All shall be well, and all shall be well, and all manner of things shall be well." So, here is a vision from heaven to comfort an earthly sufferer.

———— ❧ ————

In the year 1373, on May 13, God gave me a three-fold revelation. This was his gracious gift to me in response to my desire to know him more.

The first was a deep recollection of his passion. The second was a bodily sickness. The third was to have, of God's gift, three wounds.

As to the first, it seemed to me that I had some feeling for the Passion of Christ, but still I desired to have more by the grace of God. My wish was to have been present with those who loved Christ and were with him at his passion so that I, with my own eyes, might have seen the passion which our Lord suffered for me, and so that I might have suffered with him as the others did who loved him. I never desired any other sight or revelation of God.

To Live to Love God Better

When I was thirty years old, God sent me a bodily sickness in which I was confined to the bed for three days and nights. On the third night I received all the rites of the Church, and I did not expect to live until morning.

After this I remained in bed for two more days, and on the sixth night I thought that I was on the point of death as did those who were with me. And yet, I felt a great reluctance to die, not because of any thing on earth which held me here or because of any fear or pain, for I trusted the mercy of God. But it was because I wanted to live to love God better and longer so that I might through the grace of that living have more knowledge and love of God than I might have even in heaven!

I realized that all the time that I had lived here was very little and short in comparison with the bliss of eternal life in heaven. I thought, "Good Lord, can my living no longer be to your glory?" With all the will of my heart I assented to be wholly God's.

Hot and Flowing Freely

Then suddenly it came into my mind that I ought to wish for that first grace, that my body might be filled with a recollection of Christ's passion. It seemed to me that I might also receive the wounds which I had been praying for as well. Yet I never asked for any kind of revelation or vision from God—I only wanted to have the compassion I thought a loving soul would have for Jesus by witnessing his suffering.

It was at that moment that I saw red blood running down from under the crown, hot and flowing freely, just as it must have been beneath the crown of thorns that pressed upon his head. I fully perceived at that moment that it was Jesus, both God and man, who suffered for me, for I now knew it directly without anyone telling me.

In that same revelation, suddenly the Trinity filled my heart full of the greatest joy, and I understood that it will feel like that in heaven. For the Trinity is God; God is the Trinity. The Trinity is our maker, the Trinity is our protector, the Trinity is our everlasting lover, the Trinity is our endless joy and bliss, by our Lord Jesus Christ and in our Lord Jesus Christ.

Where Jesus appears, the blessed Trinity is understood. I said, "Blessed be the Lord!" in a loud voice. I was astonished that our God who is to be feared and revered would be so intimate with a sinful creature such as I.

Worth Thinking About

Have you ever been so sick you despaired of life? The Apostle Paul mentioned his struggle of both wishing to "depart, and to be with Christ" (Phil. 1:23) and of also wishing to remain and be responsible for the Philippians. What did he mean? Do you always pray that loved ones will be healed of their illnesses or do you pray sometimes only "thy will be done"?

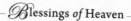

JESUS, THOU JOY OF LOVING HEARTS

Jesus, thou joy of loving hearts, Thou fount of life, thou light of men,
From the best bliss that earth imparts we turn unfilled to thee again.
Our restless spirits yearn for thee, where'er our changeful lot is cast;
Glad when thy gracious smile we see, blest when our faith
can hold thee fast.

—Bernard of Clairvaux

Prayer

DEAR FATHER, WE CANNOT ALL HAVE VISIONS OF YOU, BUT YOU DO
REVEAL YOURSELF TO US IN SCRIPTURE. HELP US TO APPRECIATE
AND LOVE YOUR WORD AND UNDERSTAND THAT YOU HAVE GIVEN US
EVERYTHING WE NEED THAT PERTAINS TO LIFE AND GODLINESS. AMEN.

Is There Any Good Reason for Believing in Life After Death?

Lee Strobel

We talk about heaven, occasionally, and there are now numerous books about people's near-death experiences—or if they were really dead, their experiences after death—and we have a literature that speaks of 'visions' of heaven. But historically what evidence do we really have for an afterlife at all unless it is related to Jesus' resurrection from the dead? After all, he is the man who came down from heaven, and he is the man who went back into heaven (see John 3:13 and Acts 1:9-10). Lee Strobel is a Christian journalist and author who specializes in the field of Christian apologetics, or evidences for the truth of the Christian faith. Before becoming a Christian, Strobel graduated from Yale Law School with a Master's Degree and wrote for *The Chicago Tribune* for many years. He became a Christian after studying the evidence for the resurrection of Jesus of Nazareth. His comments are taken from *God's Outrageous Claims: Thirteen Discoveries That Can Revolutionize Your Life* published by Zondervan in 1997.

∽∾∽

THE VERDICT OF HISTORY

If every shred of historical documentation for Jesus rising from the dead is evidence for our own eventual resurrection, we can face the future with confident expectancy. The hope that Christians will overcome the grave and spend eternity with God is not the desperate longing of people too afraid to face their own mortality. Instead, it's a rational and logical conclusion based on the compelling testimony of history.

"No intelligent jury in the world," said Lord Darling, the brilliant chief justice of England, "could fail to bring in a verdict that the Resurrection story is true."

For the Christian, that's reassuring. For spiritual seekers, that's a challenge that should be taken seriously. I've been in both camps. On a day that started out bright and beautiful in June 1983, I was glad I was in Christ's camp.

At the time, I had been working as managing editor of a newspaper in Missouri and had brought my family to Chicago to visit my mother for a few days. Late that night, I got up feeling ill and promptly collapsed in tremendous pain.

My wife called the paramedics. As they were on their way, I was sprawled on the floor—my breathing shallow, my pulse erratic, my skin pale—fighting to stay conscious and feeling an ominous numbness creep up my arms and legs. "This is it," I thought to myself. I figured I was going to die just like my friend Frank had several years earlier.

I'll admit it: I was scared. I didn't want to die. I wanted to see my children grow up. I wanted to live a long and happy life with Leslie. But I had been a Christian for about eighteen months, and I knew with certainty that I could trust two things if I died: first, that God would watch over Leslie and the kids: second, that the moment I closed my eyes in death, I would reopen them in the presence of God.

And Jesus would put his arm around me and say to the Father, "I know this man. I love him, and he loves me. I've paid for every single sin he ever committed. On the merits of what I did on the cross, he is washed clean of all wrongdoing and clothed in my goodness—and therefore invited to spend eternity in heaven."

I was in a win-win situation: if I lived, everything would be fine, and if I died, everything would be fine. That gave me the kind of courage I needed to cope with the crisis.

Obviously I didn't die. After nearly a week in the hospital, during which doctors were never quite able to diagnose the malady that had stricken me that night, I emerged to experience lots of other bright and beautiful days. But sooner or later one of them will be my last. Death still stalks me, as it does you.

But we can proceed with bold assurance, thanks to the evidence of history that establishes with convincing clarity how Jesus not only preceded us in death but also came back from the dead and blazed the trail to heaven.

"I write these things to you who believe in the name of the Son of God," said the apostle John, "so that you may *know* that you have eternal life." [1 John 5:13, emphasis added]

Worth Thinking About

Have you ever considered what sound evidence there is for the resurrection? What number of witnesses there were to it? Thomas's examination of the risen Christ? The wonder of the women at the tomb? We can't examine a piece of heaven, but we have the words of the man who came from heaven and went back to heaven to count on about its existence and beauty. What more evidence could we want?

ABIDE WITH ME

Abide with me: fast falls the eventide;

The darkness deepens; Lord, with me abide:

When other helpers fail, and comforts flee,

Help of the helpless, O abide with me!
Hold Thou Thy cross before my closing eyes,
Shine through the gloom, and point me to the skies:
Heaven's morning breaks, and earth's vain shadows flee—
In life, in death, O Lord, abide with me!

—H. F. Lyte

rayer

DEAR FATHER, HELP US TO LIVE LIKE CITIZENS OF HEAVEN NOW, FULL
OF CONVICTION THAT WILL CAUSE OTHERS TO FOLLOW YOUR WAY.
ALTHOUGH DEATH IS AN EVERYDAY REALITY, HELP US TO SEE IT IS NOT
THE END, BUT ONLY THE BEGINNING OF LIFE ETERNAL. AMEN.

What's Important in Heaven: the Quality or Quantity of My Works?

Charles R. Swindoll

Charles R. Swindoll's radio program "Insights for Living" has been a mainstay of Christian broadcasting for more than fifty years, and Swindoll has published some seventy books, many of them best sellers. Additionally, he is Chancellor of Dallas Theological Seminary and senior pastor at Stonebriar Community Church in Frisco, Texas. His book, from which this article is taken, is *The Finishing Touch: Becoming God's Masterpiece*, published by Word Publishing in 1994.

~∞∞~

One of the great doctrines of Christianity is our belief in a heavenly home. Ultimately, we shall spend eternity with God in the place He has prepared for us. And part of that exciting anticipation is His promise to reward His servants for a job well done. Scripture not only supports the idea of eternal rewards, it spells out the specifics. I find three primary facts about rewards in 1 Corinthians 3:10-14.

Most rewards are received in heaven, not on earth. Now don't misunderstand. There are earthly rewards. But when it comes to servanthood, God reserves special honor for that day when "each man's work will become evident" and "he shall receive a reward" (3:13-14).

All rewards are based on quality, not quantity. We humans are impressed with size and volume and noise and numbers.

It is easy to forget that God's eye is always on motive. When He rewards servants, it will be based on *quality*—which means everybody has an equal opportunity to receive a reward. The elderly woman who prays before an audience of one will be rewarded as much as the evangelist who preaches before an audience of thousands.

No reward that is postponed will be forgotten. God doesn't settle His accounts at the end of every day. Nor does He close out His books toward the end of everyone's life. But when that day in eternity dawns, when time shall be no more on this earth, no act of serving others—be it well-known or unknown to others—will be forgotten. Unlike many people today, God keeps His promises.

Someone once counted all the promises in the Bible and came up with an amazing figure of almost 7500. Among that large number are some specific promises servants can claim today. Believe me, there are times when the only thing that will keep you going is a promise from God that your work is not in vain.

When we have done what was needed, but were ignored, misunderstood, or forgotten . . . we can be sure it was not in vain.

When we did what was right, with the right motive, but received no credit, no acknowledgment, not even a "thank you" . . . we have God's promise that "we shall reap."

When any servant has served and given and sacrificed and then willingly stepped aside for God to receive the glory, our heavenly Father promises he will receive back.

Among the temporal rewards we will receive is the *quiet awareness that the life of Christ is being modeled.* I know of few more satisfying and encouraging rewards than the realization that our actions are a visible expression of Christ to others.

Another temporal reward is the *joyful realization that a thankful spirit is being stimulated.* "All this is for your benefit, so that the grace that is reaching more and more people may cause thanksgiving to overflow to the glory of God" (2 Cor. 4:15 NIV).

———

Worth Thinking About

All along in the sacred story there has been God's promise of reward for our service to him. Everything from God issues from grace which is a gift, and the rewards are a gift too, because God is generous in his love and pleasure with his children. If our earthly parents have been generous with us, how much more will our heavenly Father be? But do we bring the same quality control goals to work for heaven that we do for our earthly work? A song pleads "give of your best to the Master"? Is that what we are doing?

GIVE OF YOUR BEST TO THE MASTER

Give of your best to the Master;

Give of the strength of your youth;

Throw your soul's fresh glowing ardor

Into the battle for truth.

Jesus has set the example,

Dauntless was he, young and brave;

Give him your loyal devotion;

Give him the best that you have.

—Howard B. Grose

Prayer

DEAR FATHER, YOU TAKE OUR LITTLE SERVICE AND REWARD US GREATLY. HELP US TO NOT FORGET EITHER THE CROSS OR THE MANY WAYS YOU UPHOLD US AND HELP US TO SERVE YOU. MOST OF ALL, THANK YOU FOR JESUS, OUR FRIEND AND LORD TO WHOM QUALITY SERVICE IS OWED. AMEN.

If Life Itself Has Been a Struggle, Will Eternal Life Be Any Better?

Randy Alcorn

"Each day has enough trouble of its own," (Matt. 6:24) our Lord Jesus observed. Critics have contradicted our Lord's sayings on many matters, but few have felt the need to contradict him on this one. Randy Alcorn, founder of Eternal Perspective Ministries, believes that the best is yet to be, and that dreams unfulfilled in this life will finally come to pass in the life to come. What do you think? This selection is from Alcorn's bestselling book *Heaven*.

⁂

Many people believe this life is all there is. Their philosophy? "You only go around once on this earth, so grab for whatever you can."

If you're a child of God, you do *not* just "go around once" on Earth. You don't get just one earthly life. You get another—one far better and without end. You'll inhabit the New Earth! You'll live with the God you cherish and the people you love as an undying person on an undying Earth. Those who go to Hell are the ones who go around only once on this earth.

We use the term eternal life without thinking what it means. . . . Eternal life will be enjoying forever what life on Earth is at its finest moments, what it was intended to be. Since in Heaven we'll finally experience life at its best, it would be more accurate to call our present existence the *beforelife* rather than what follows the *afterlife*.

WILL UNFULFILLED DREAMS BE REALIZED IN HEAVEN?

Without an eternal perspective, without understanding the reality that the best is yet to come, we assume that people who die young, who are handicapped, who aren't healthy, who don't get married, or who don't _____ [fill in the blank] will inevitably miss out on the best life has to offer. . . .

What are we thinking?

One day Nanci [his wife—Ed.] read me letters we'd never before seen translated, written in 1920 by her grandmother Ana Swanson to her family in Sweden. Ana suffered severe health problems. While she was in Montana, cared for by relatives, her husband, Edwin, was in Oregon, working and caring for their seven children day and night. Ana's letters tell how Edwin wore himself out, got sick, and died. Because Ana was too weak to care for her younger children, they, including Nanci's mother, Adele, were given up for adoption. Ana's letters reflect her broken heart, her nagging guilt . . . and her faith in God.

Nanci and I were overcome with tears as we read those letters. What tragic lives. What inconsolable disappointment and pain. Ana and Edwin loved Jesus. They once had great dreams for their lives and family. But poor health, misfortune, separation, and death forever stripped them of each other, their children, and their dreams.

Or did it?

As Nanci and I talked, we considered what God might choose to give this broken family on the New Earth. Perhaps they'll go together to places they would have gone if health and finances had allowed. Certainly Ana won't be plagued by illness, fatigue, grief, anxiety, and guilt. Isn't it likely their gracious God, who delights in redemption and renewal and restoration, will give them wonderful family times they were robbed of on the old Earth? Perhaps the God of second chances won't merely comfort Ana by removing her grief for what she lost. Perhaps he will in some way actually restore what she lost. Our God won't just take away suffering; he'll compensate by giving us greater delights than if there had been no suffering. . . . Hence, "our present sufferings are not worth comparing with the glory that will be revealed in us" (Romans 8:18).

Worth Thinking About

Sometimes when we read John 10:10—"I have come that they may have life, and have it to the full"—we are tempted to think that that means smooth sailing, clear skies, and that we will get everything we wish for in this life. This view nowhere squares with the real life that Paul and the other apostles had. Indeed, a certain amount of trouble is promised to those who follow Jesus (see Mark 10:29-30). How can we encourage those Christians who aren't seeing much of heaven's blessing now? Are we willing to stand with them in their trials?

BLESSED ARE YOU

> Looking at his disciples, he said: "Blessed are you who are poor, for yours is the kingdom of God. Blessed are you who hunger now, for you will be satisfied. Blessed are you who weep now, for you will laugh. Blessed are you when men hate you, when they exclude you and insult you and reject your name as evil, because of the Son of Man. Rejoice in that day and leap for joy, because great is your reward in heaven" (Luke 6:20-23a NIV).

rayer

DEAR FATHER, HELP US TO BELIEVE IT WILL 'BE WORTH IT ALL' WHEN WE GO TO HEAVEN AND GIVE US IMAGINATIONS TO INSPIRE OTHERS WHO ARE WEARY ALONG THE WAY. HELP US TO LIVE KNOWING THAT THOSE WHO ARE HUMBLED IN THIS LIFE WILL BE EXALTED IN THE WORLD TO COME. AMEN.

WILL OUR SOULS FALL ASLEEP UNTIL THE RESURRECTION OF THE DEAD?

Wilbur M. Smith (1894-1977)

Dr. Wilbur M. Smith was, for many years, Professor of English Bible at Fuller Theological Seminary, which he helped to found. Before that he had taught for eleven years at Moody Bible Institute without having ever actually graduated from a seminary (he briefly attended Dallas Theological Seminary). The author of sixty books, he finished his teaching career as Professor of Biblical Studies at Trinity Evangelical Divinity School. In 1968 Dr. Smith wrote the groundbreaking *The Biblical Doctrine of Heaven,* published by Moody Press, which attempted to break a sort of theological silence about heaven that had developed early in the twentieth century and continued well into the fifties. Few people were asking questions about the specifics of heaven then, but Dr. Smith helped to change that. Does the soul fall asleep at death as a few theologians have taught down through the ages or is it forever alive? Here are Dr. Smith's insights in the following passages.

⸺⸻⸺

The idea that the soul goes immediately into the presence of the Lord upon death is implied in the famous words of the apostle: "But I am in a strait betwixt two, having a desire to depart, and to be with Christ; which is far better: nevertheless to abide in the flesh is more needful for you" (Phil. 1:23-24). Some of the very words used in the New Testament imply the conscious continuance of the soul after death has separated it from the body. Those appearing to our Lord on the mount of transfiguration spoke to Christ concerning His decease (Luke 9:31). The Greek word used here, *exodos,* is also used by the Apostle Peter, referring to his coming death (II Peter 1:15). The word is used of the actual exodus of the children of Israel from Egypt (Heb. 11:22). They certainly did not go into a state of slumber when they entered into the wilderness of Sinai. . . .

We cannot of course attempt a fairly comprehensive study of what is known as the intermediate state without giving very careful attention to a passage of the Apostle Paul in his second letter to the Corinthians that probably has had more different interpretations than any other extended eschatological passage in all of Paul's writings. After speaking of having been in a state of danger, perplexed but not despairing, smitten down but not destroyed, bearing about in the body the dying of Jesus, he was nevertheless fully assured that God who "raised up the Lord Jesus shall raise up us also with Jesus, and shall present us with you." He then concludes with one of his most glorious utterances: "Wherefore we faint not; but though our outward man is decaying, yet our inward man is renewed day by day. For our light affliction, which is for the moment, worketh for us more and more exceedingly an eternal weight of glory; while we look not at the things which are seen, but at the things which are not seen: for the things which are seen are temporal; but the things which are not seen are eternal" (II Cor. 4:16-18). It is in this context that we find this passage on the intermediate state, if it is such, concerning which so many interpretations have been offered. "For we know that if the earthly house of our tabernacle be dissolved, we have a building from God, a house not made with hands, eternal, in the heavens. For in this we groan, longing to be clothed upon with our habitation which is from heaven: if so be that being clothed we shall not be found naked.

For indeed we that are in this tabernacle do groan, being burdened; not for that we would be unclothed, but that we would be clothed upon, that what is mortal may be swallowed up of life. Now he that wrought us for this very thing is God, who gave unto us the earnest of the Spirit" (II Cor. 5:1-5). . . .

Whatever be the interpretation of this Corinthian passage, we would repeat that the church throughout the ages normally has held the view that the soul at the time of death enters into the presence of the Lord. . . .

This well-known statement of the *Westminster Confession of Faith* (chap. XXXII) reads as follows:

The bodies of men after death return to dust, and see corruption; but their souls, (which neither die nor sleep,) having an immortal subsistence, immediately return to God who gave them. The souls of the righteous, being then made perfect in holiness, are received into the highest heavens, where they behold the face of God in light and glory, waiting for the full redemption of their bodies. . . .

Worth Thinking About

Perhaps, after all, it is the body that does the sleeping in the ground or wherever the body has perished. What do you think? The church continues to struggle to this very day with Paul's statement that to be absent from the body is to be present with the Lord. Yet, at the same time, the church acknowledges, and has always acknowledged, there will be a resurrection of all the dead at the end of the age. Maybe this is a case where God's ways are not our ways, and the resurrection of the Lord's children will then be the complete fulfillment of what Christ did for us at Calvary.

REDEEMED FROM DEATH

Be Thou my rock, my dwelling place, forever mine, as now;
Salvation Thou hast willed for me, my rock and fortress, Thou.
Redeemed, redeemed, by Thee redeemed from death;
My soul shall give Thee joyful praise, redeemed, redeemed from death.

—Anonymous

*P*rayer

DEAR FATHER, THANK YOU FOR WHAT WE KNOW OF ETERNAL LIFE NOW AND OF WHAT YOU HAVE CHOSEN NOT TO REVEAL. HELP US TO BE CURIOUS BUT PATIENT THAT WE MAY GROW IN FAITH. WE ASK THAT WE'D CONTINUE TO TAKE COMFORT IN THE TRUTH OF YOUR PRESENCE WITH US IN THIS LIFE AND IN THE LIFE TO COME. AMEN.

HAVE YOU EVER FELT THE STIRRING OF GOD'S HEAVENLY SPIRIT?

Joni Eareckson Tada

Relatively few Christians claim to have had actual glimpses of heaven such as the deacon Stephen was granted in Acts 7:56: "Behold, I see the heavens opened up and the Son of Man standing at the right hand of God" (NASB). But many believers feel they've had glimpses of God's glory through the beauty to be found in nature and personal experiences of what might be called "divine moments." Can you identify with Joni Eareckson Tada's recollection from her childhood? "I knew my heart had been broken by God." This passage comes from her book *Heaven: Your Real Home*.

A FIRST HINT OF HEAVEN

The first time I heard that hauntingly heavenly song [an intimation of heaven—Ed.], so ancient and so new, was the summer of 1957. My family and I had packed up, piled into our old Buick, and were heading west through the country roads of Kansas. Daddy pulled the car over onto the gravel shoulder to stop by a roadside ditch so my sister could go to the bathroom. I jumped out of the sweltering backseat and wandered beside a barbed wire fence along the road. It was a chance to dry the sweat off my back, as well as to explore.

I stopped and picked up a piece of gravel, examined it, and then heaved the stone beyond the fence far out into the biggest, widest, longest field I had ever seen. It was an ocean of wheat, waves of golden grain rippling in the wind, all broad and beautiful against a brilliant blue sky. I stood and stared. A warm breeze tossed my hair. A butterfly flittered. Except for the hissing sound of summertime bugs, all was quiet, incredibly quiet.

Or was it?

I can't remember if the song came from the sky or the field, or if it was just the sound of crickets. I tried hard to listen, but instead of actually hearing notes, I felt . . . space. A wide-open space filling my heart, as if the entire wheat field could fit into my seven-year-old soul. I rolled my head back to look up at a hawk circling overhead. The bird, sky, sun, and field were lifting me in some heavenly orchestration, lightening my heart with honesty and clarity like an American folk hymn in a major key, pure, upright, and vertical. I had never felt—or was it, heard?—such a thing.

I was only seven, but standing there by the barbed wire fence of a Kansas wheat field, I knew my heart had been broken by God. No, I didn't actually know Him at the time, but I wasn't so young that I couldn't sense the occasional stirrings of His Spirit. I kept staring while humming an old Sunday school favorite: "This world is not my home, I'm just a-passin' through." For me, the moment was heavenly.

Daddy honked the horn and I ran back. Our family drove away with a slightly changed little girl in the backseat.

Worth Thinking About

Any experience no matter how unique or even odd that draws you closer to Jesus is evidence of the Spirit of God working in you (see John 14:14-15 and Phil. 2:13). Do you agree with or feel uncomfortable with this statement? Where might it be taken too far? Does the Holy Spirit work in people's lives before they come to know Christ? What is your own experience in these matters?

OPEN MY EYES, THAT I MAY SEE

Open My Eyes, That I May See glimpses of truth thou hast for me;
Place in my hands the wonderful key that shall unclasp and set me free.
Silently now I wait for thee, ready, my God, thy will to see;
Open my eyes, illumine me, Spirit divine!

—Clara H. Scott

Prayer

DEAR FATHER, WE EARNESTLY SEEK THAT YOU WOULD CONTINUE TO WORK IN OUR LIVES. HELP US TO BE ALERT TO THE MANY WAYS IN WHICH YOU WITNESS TO US THROUGH OTHER BELIEVERS AND THROUGH YOUR CREATED WORLD. CREATE IN US A HEART TENDER TOWARD YOUR MESSAGE. AMEN.

How Can We Encourage Others on Their Journey to Heaven?

Anne Dutton (1692-1765)

Information on British Baptist Anne Dutton is scarce. Her surviving work is simply titled *Letters on Spiritual Subjects*. The circumstances of her life have conspired to keep her contributions to Christian literature pretty much in the shadows. Religious leaders of her day were somewhat concerned that she, as a woman, would even be writing on Christian doctrine, and she was subject to some criticism for doing so. However, she did correspond with George Whitfield and John Wesley and was not unlearned in spiritual matters; rather she was self-taught. Dutton eventually became a sort of spiritual director for those who sought her advice. Here follows an excellent example of how we might develop a ministry of encouragement to those of our brothers and sisters who are finding the journey long and the way wearying.

My very Dear Sister in the Lord,

We are almost home! A few more trials, and then farewell, trials, forever! The bosom of Christ, the glory of the heavenly state is ready for us [Rev. 21:3-4]. In a little while, we shall be fully made fit to be partakers of the inheritance of the saints in light [Col. 1:12]. Do not grieve that you are left alone, and have few friends that you can open your heart to, for your dear Lord Jesus will never leave nor forsake you [Heb. 13:5]; and He is a friend that sticks closer than a brother [Prov. 18:24]. You have had sweet experience of Christ's friendship ever since you were first acquainted with Him; and His love towards you, His care for you, and His power to save you are still as great as ever.

Time has not altered Christ's heart; no, nor all the weaknesses and provocations He has seen in you, but having loved you anciently, freely, and fully, He will love you eternally [Rom. 8:31-32]. Your Jesus, your best Friend, who has cared for you all along, will never cast you off. He has engraved you upon the palms of His hands [Isa. 49:16], and your walls are continually before Him. Creatures may forget—the tenderest mother may forget her nursing child—but your Jesus, in His boundless compassions, will not, cannot forget you. He will know your soul in adversity, when all other refuges fail you, and no man cares for your soul.

As birds flying to support and defend their young, so will the Lord make haste to help you, for *His care for you is infinite,* and He will keep you as the apple of His eye [Ps. 17:8]. You are one of Christ's jewels, and His heart is the cabinet in which He will keep you; and from His heart-care of you, His providential care for you shall be shown. And as to the *power* of Christ, He is the Lord Almighty, and His everlasting arms will never grow weary of bearing you and all your burdens [see Deut. 33:27]. The Lord well knew that His people would need to be dandled by Him and carried by Him for a long while—that they would at times be subject to fears, from their own weakness and unworthiness, and from the occurrence of new difficulties; and from hence that they would be anxious how they would get the rest of their way through the wilderness. And therefore he says, "Hearken unto me, O house of Jacob, and all the remnant of the house of Israel, which are borne by me from the belly, which are carried from the womb: and even to your old age I am he; and even to hoar hairs will I carry you: I have made, and I will bear; *even I will carry, and will deliver you*" (Isaiah 46:3, 4).

Oh, my dear sister, there is grace enough in this promise to carry you safely and comfortably through all your remaining trials, even down to death and up to glory. Therefore, trust in the Lord forever, for in the Lord Jehovah is everlasting strength. He is your ever-living and ever-loving Friend. Live upon Him for all in all, and as your all, and in all things labor to live to Him; so shall the name of our Lord Jesus be glorified in you, and you in Him, according to the Will of God and our Father.

Our dear Lord is exceedingly kind to unworthy me. He heaps favors upon me, and surrounds me with mercies, because He will be gracious—even to me, a poor, vile, hell-deserving sinner. Oh, it is well for us that grace reigns through the righteousness of Jesus, and that we, receiving abundance of grace, shall reign with Him [Rev. 5:10]. Oh, bless the Lord with me, and let us exalt His name together for all His great goodness, and His wonderful works for poor, sinful me [Ps. 34:3]. And pray for me, that I may be made holiness unto the Lord, very fruitful to the glory of His name, and very useful to His dear and tender lambs. All glory to my dear Lord! Oh, how great and many have been the precious thoughts of God's kindness towards me of old, which daily open in new wonders to my view!

I wish you a rich increase of all grace and peace, through the once slain, now reigning Lamb [Rev. 5:9-10]!

Worth Thinking About

We have more capacity to communicate with our family, friends, and neighbors than at any time in history, and heaven is closer to each of us now than ever before—and comes closer with each passing minute! Who do you know who needs an encouraging word? Can you take

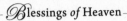

time in your day to just drop a note, email, text message—or even call—to tell someone there is hope stored up in heaven for him or her where Christ continually prays on their behalf?

THOU ART WORTHY

> And they sung a new song, saying, thou art worthy to take the book, and to open the seals thereof: for thou wast slain and hast redeemed us to God by thy blood out of every kindred, and tongue, and people, and nation; and hast made us unto our God kings and priests: and we shall reign on the earth.—Revelation 5:9-10

Prayer

DEAR FATHER, HELP US TO BE ENCOURAGED AND TO KNOW THAT OUR LABOR IS NOT IN VAIN IN YOU. HELP US TO KNOW WHO THOSE ARE WHO NEED AN ENCOURAGING WORD AND GIVE US INSIGHT INTO HOW TO GIVE IT. AMEN.

How Do the Angels of Heaven Act for Us Now on Earth?

Wilbur M. Smith (1894-1977)

Wilbur M. Smith was one of the most important biblical expositors of the twentieth century. His influence has largely waned today, although he was one of the founders of Fuller Theological Seminary and had thirty-three years of teaching ministry at Moody Bible Institute, Fuller Seminary, and Trinity Evangelical Divinity School. Perhaps his most famous book was *Therefore Stand,* which marked an important milestone in the history of evangelical apologetics. *The Biblical Doctrine of Heaven,* from which this excerpt comes, was a landmark book published by Moody Press in 1968. Before that time, very few books on the subject of heaven had been written for twentieth century readers, and as for angels, they were even less written about. However, if angels were active in the early church, there is no reason to believe they are any less active today.

∞∞∞

On two different occasions our Lord refers to the fact that when He returns to this earth it will be with His angels, or in detail, it will be an event in which "the holy angels" are with Him (Matt. 16:27; 25:31; Mark 8:38). Once again He refers to the fact that "he shall send forth his angels with a great sound of a trumpet, and they shall gather together his elect from the four winds, from one end of heaven to the other" (Matt. 24:31). . . .

While the angelic ministry in the book of Acts has received considerable attention [throughout Christian history—Ed.], the data does not particularly add to what we already know about angelic activity. Twice angels released an apostle from prison (5:19: 12:7 ff.). It is an angel that commanded Philip to go down to Gaza (8:26). Cornelius' great experience in being converted to the gospel began when "he saw in a vision openly, as it were about the ninth hour of the day, an angel of God coming in unto him" (10:3). Finally, at the end of that terrible experience in the storm on the Mediterranean, Paul told the entire crew of the ship, "There stood by me this night an angel of the God whose I am, whom also I serve, saying, Fear not, Paul: thou must stand before Caesar: and lo, God hath granted thee all them that sail with thee" (27:23-24).

When St. Peter, released from prison, came to the home of Mary, the mother of Mark, and rapped upon the door, the maid reported that Peter was at the gate, but they refused to believe her and remarked, "It is his angel."

This may well be the place to ask the question, Are guardian angels assigned to redeemed individuals? It has been insisted upon by many that such guardian angels are to be assumed. The passage generally quoted is the famous utterance of our Lord in referring to little children: "I say unto you that in heaven their angels do always behold the face of my Father who is in heaven" (Matt. 18:10). Many decades ago, one of America's most careful scholars, Moses Stuart, in arguing for guardian angels, remarked on this passage:

In what other way can we reasonably interpret this, except as assigning to little children . . . angels of the highest order (comp. Isaiah 6:2 sq. and Revelation 1:4), as their guardians and protectors . . . ?

The famous German exegete Hermann Cremer even went further into detail in saying, "The angels of God bear their souls thither where Christ has preceded them to heaven, the place of eternal life and of the glory of God, there to be till they and all saints shall be revealed from thence with Christ."

Worth Thinking About

It can be argued that we have nothing from Scripture that says individual adults each have a guardian angel, but neither can it be maintained that we need less angelic protection than do children just because we have grown older. What do you think? What other passages of Scripture reveal what agents from heaven are doing on our behalf? What pattern and purpose do you see when God sent his messengers to intervene in history?

"I AM YOUR FELLOW SERVANT"

> Now I, John, saw and heard these things. And when I heard and saw, I fell down to worship before the feet of the angel who showed me these things. Then he said to me, "See that you do not do that. For I am your fellow servant, and of your brethren the prophets, and of those who keep the words of this book. Worship God."—Revelation 22:8-9

Prayer

DEAR FATHER, WE OFTEN SEE THROUGH A GLASS DARKLY, AND THOUGH WE DO NOT KNOW MUCH ABOUT HOW YOUR MINISTERING ANGELS WORK FOR YOU ON OUR BEHALF, WE THANK YOU FOR THEIR HUMBLE SERVICE AND EXAMPLE. MAY WE BE AS COMMITTED TO YOUR HOLY WILL AS THEY ARE. AMEN.

WHAT DOES THE SYMBOLIC LANGUAGE OF HEAVEN TELL US ABOUT JESUS?

John Ortberg

Confused about the language used to describe our Lord in Heaven? You aren't the only one. Yet there is much that we can know through symbolic words used of Jesus in the Book of Revelation, as pastor John Ortberg here explains from his book *Everybody Is Normal Till You Get to Know Them,* published by Zondervan in 2003. Do you think his interpretation helps you understand some of the difficult passages in Revelation? Do we need to understand every symbol to benefit from heavenly words of comfort?

—∞∞∞—

HEAVEN IS A PERSON

Trapped on the island of Patmos, John has a vision of the throne room of heaven. It is a strange vision of one "like a son of man," with hair that is white like wool, eyes that blaze like fire, a double-edged sword coming out of his mouth, and hands holding the stars of the churches and the keys to death and Hades.

John falls down before the person's feet as though dead, and the "son of man"—who is, indeed, the Son of Man—touches him with his right hand and says, "Do not be afraid. I am the First and the Last. I am the Living One; I was dead, and behold I am alive for ever and ever . . . !" [Rev. 1:18]

God has all the wisdom we associate with age, except that he is eternal. Yet, one day all the wisdom he has will be put at our disposal. We will never again say a foolish word or make a wrong decision. We will be guided by pure wisdom.

The Son of Man also holds seven stars in his hand. His *right* hand [Rev. 1:16]. This means the figure is ready for action. The right side was considered most noble. That is why a powerful man was called the right-hand man of a king and why a soldier with a sword in his right hand was ready to fight. . . .

The stars are associated with the messengers, or angels, of the churches to whom John is writing: John is saying that the churches are perfectly safe in the hand of God. . . .

The man has a sword sticking out of his mouth. This is a strange image to us. It does not mean that when we see Jesus one day, he will have a blade between his lips. In John's day, a sword was the symbol of power. To have a sword coming from the mouth is a way of saying that the word of the Son of Man carries unstoppable authority. He speaks, and it is so.

This is why John gives this person that great title "the ruler of the kings of the earth." In our day, we experience separate spheres of power: political, economic, cultural, and so on. In Jesus' day, kings held all the power. And Jesus is the ruler over the kings.

To put it in our terms, think of all the holders of power in every sphere in our day—all the movers and shakers and opinion molders. Jesus is ruler over them all, whether they know it or not, Jesus is ruler over presidents and prime ministers, over statesmen and party hacks. He is ruler over Democrats and Republicans. . . .

These people and powers may not realize now that Jesus is ruler, but the day is coming when they will—maybe today, maybe tomorrow—but it is coming. On that day, "every knee will bow"—even the most proud and stubborn. Every tongue will "confess that Jesus Christ is Lord" [Phil. 2:10-11]—Lord of Lords and ruler of the kings of the earth.

This is the holy, transcendent, awe-inspiring figure John sees in his vision. And then things get serious.

John says that when he saw this figure, he "fell at his feet as though dead." No wonder! He is overcome by the distance that separates a sinful human being from a holy God. John falls at Jesus' feet in awe, wonder, fear, and utter surrender. He is undone.

Then comes one of the most wonderful moments in Scripture. John says, "He placed his right hand on me."

Imagine falling as if dead at Jesus' feet and having him take that all-powerful right hand, empty now, and place it on your shoulder.

"Don't be afraid," he says, "I'm the one you saw who died, yet lives."

---

*W*orth Thinking About

Jesus is ruler now over all his creation Ortberg says, yet we do not always find it possible to see that. In what way is God "doing something" now about the sad conditions of the world, and how can we make his rule known to our neighbors? In what way is God "ruler over Democrats and Republicans"?

THE PROMISED HOLY SPIRIT

God has raised this Jesus to life, and we are all witnesses of the fact. Exalted to the right hand of God, he has received from the Father the promised Holy Spirit and has poured out what you now see and hear. For David did not ascend to heaven, and yet he said,

'The Lord said to my Lord:
Sit at my right hand until I make your enemies a

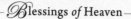

footstool for your feet.' Therefore let all Israel be assured of this: God has made this Jesus, whom you crucified, both Lord and Christ. —Acts 2:32-35

DEAR FATHER, HELP US TO LET YOU REIGN IN OUR HEARTS SO THAT YOUR WILL MAY BE SEEN ON EARTH. ALSO, HELP US TO BELIEVE THAT YOUR RULE GOES ON EVEN WHEN WE DON'T SEE IT AND EVEN WHEN WRONG SEEMS TO PREVAIL. HELP US TO LIFT UP JESUS THAT ALL MIGHT BE DRAWN TO HIM. AMEN.

Does Having a Heavenly Treasure in Earthen Vessels Dim Our View of the Future?

John Wesley (1703-1791)

John Wesley would have been on the list of the most important people in England, had there been a magazine to make such a list in his day. Some historians claim the founder of Methodism saved his country from the terrors of the French Revolution by speaking in the open fields to the masses and giving them a hope in Christ that was not provided by England's class-restricted society. Having a heavenly treasure in earthen vessels does not mean we can know nothing of heaven now but only that our experience is clouded by earthly dimness. This excerpt from the sermon "Heavenly Treasure in Earthen Vessels" was published in a collection of Wesley's work in 1872.

❦

"We have this treasure in earthen vessels."—2 Corinthians 4:7

May we not believe, that all Christians, though but nominally such, have sometimes at least, some desire to please God, as well as some light concerning what does really please him, and some convictions when they are sensible of displeasing him? Such treasure have all the children of men, more or less, even when they do not yet know God.

But it is not these of whom the Apostle is here speaking; neither is this the treasure which is the subject of his discourse. The persons concerning whom he is here speaking are those that are born of God; those that, "being justified by faith," have now redemption in the blood of Jesus, even the forgiveness of sins; those who enjoy that peace of God which passes all understanding; whose soul does magnify the Lord, and rejoice in him with joy unspeakable; and who feel the "love of God shed abroad in their hearts by the Holy Ghost, which is given unto them." [Rom. 5:5] This, then, is the treasure which they have received; — a faith of the operation of God; a peace which sets them above the fear of death, and enables them in everything to be content; an hope full of immortality, whereby they already "taste of the powers of the world to come;" the love of God shed abroad in their hearts with love to every child of man, and a renewal in the whole image of God, in all righteousness and true holiness. This is properly and directly the treasure concerning which the Apostle is here speaking.

But this, invaluable as it is, "we have in earthen vessels." The word is exquisitely proper, denoting both the brittleness of the vessels, and the meanness of the matter they are made of. It directly means what we term earthenware: china, porcelain, and the like. How weak, how easily broken in pieces! Just such is the case with a holy Christian. We have the heavenly treasure in earthly, mortal, corruptible bodies. "Dust thou art," said the righteous Judge to his rebellious creature, till then incorruptible and immortal, "and to dust thou shalt return." [Gen. 3:19] How finely (but with what a mixture of light and darkness) does the heathen poet touch upon this change! *Post ignem etherea domo subduxerat,* — "After man had stolen fire from heaven," (what an emblem of forbidden knowledge!) *macies et nova febrium,* etc.—that unknown army of consumptions, fevers, sickness, pain of every kind, fixed their camp upon earth, which till then they could no more have entered than they could scale heaven; and all tended to introduce and pave the way for the last enemy, death. From the moment that awful sentence was pronounced the body received the sentence of death in itself; if not from the moment our first parents completed their rebellion by eating of the forbidden fruit. May we not probably conjecture that there was some quality naturally in this, which sowed the seeds of death in the human body, till then incorruptible and immortal? Be this as it may, it is certain that, from this time, "the corruptible body has pressed down the soul. . . ."

But suppose it pleased the all-wise Creator, for the sin of man, to suffer the souls of men in general to be weighed down in this miserable manner by their corruptible body; why does he permit the excellent treasure which he has entrusted to his own children to be still lodged in these poor "earthen vessels?" Would not this question naturally occur to any reflecting mind? Perhaps it would; and therefore the Apostle immediately furnishes us with a full answer: God has done this, that "the excellency of the power might be of God, and not of us;" that it might be undeniably plain to whom that excellent power belonged; that no flesh might glory in his sight; but that all who have received this treasure might continually cry, "Not unto us, but unto thee, O Lord, be the praise, for thy name and for thy truth's sake." [Ps. 115:1]

Undoubtedly this was the main design of God in this wonderful dispensation; to humble man, to make and keep him little and poor, and base, and vile, in his own eyes. . . .

Come on then, disease, weakness, pain,—afflictions, in the language of men. Shall we not be infinite gainers by them? Gainers for ever and ever! Seeing "these light afflictions, which are but for a moment, work out for us a far more exceeding and eternal weight of glory!" [2 Cor. 4:17]

And are we not, by the consciousness of our present weakness, effectually taught wherein our strength lies? How loud does it proclaim, "Trust in the Lord Jehovah; for in him is ever-lasting strength!" [Ps. 73:28] Trust in Him who suffered a thousand times more than ever you can suffer! Has he not all power in heaven and in earth?

> The heavenly treasure now we have
> In a vile house of clay!
> But Christ shall to the utmost save,
> And keep us to that day.
>
> —Charles Wesley

———

*W*orth Thinking About

There is a glory that is to be revealed when we are transformed into our new heavenly bodies, yet even now some of Christ's glory is shown when we serve him. Do we see more of Christ in some of his children than in others? Who are some of your heroes in gospel faithfulness? What can we do to let our "light shine before men" so that they may glorify God (Matt. 5:16)?

LIVING FOR JESUS

> O Jesus, Lord and Savior, I give myself to Thee;
> For Thou, in Thy atonement, didst give Thyself for me;
> I own no other Master, my heart shall by Thy Throne,
> My life I give, henceforth to live, O Christ, for Thee alone.
>
> —Thomas O. Chisholm

Prayer

DEAR FATHER, HELP US KNOW THAT OTHERS ARE ALWAYS WATCHING US, AND MAY THEY SEE CHRIST OUR LORD LIVING IN US. YET MAY WE GLADLY ACCEPT OUR EARTHEN BODIES FOR WHAT THEY ARE IN THE EXPECTATION OF THE GLORY OF OUR NEW BODIES PROMISED US LONG AGO. THANK YOU THAT CHRIST'S NEW BODY FORESHADOWS WHAT OURS WILL BE. AMEN.

Do We Deserve the Gift of Heaven?

Richard Baxter (1615–1691)

According to the Puritan divine Richard Baxter, we do not deserve the gift of heaven. Quite the contrary, we deserve the place of separation from God but are freely given a place of fellowship and rest with him on the merits of Christ alone. Furthermore, Baxter, a theologian, poet, and hymn-writer, believed that salvation was genuinely offered to all, and in this he departed from his Calvinist brothers. C. S. Lewis found Baxter an excellent theologian and used Baxter's phrase "mere Christian" in the title of his most famous book, *Mere Christianity*. For Baxter, mere Christianity is all about the work of Christ on our behalf where we receive a surpassing gift we definitely do *not* deserve! This excerpt comes from Baxter's own classic *The Saints' Everlasting Rest* published about 1650.

⚬⚬⚬

Let us draw a little nearer and see the splendor of this heavenly rest. The Lord covers us with His gentle grace while we approach to take this view.

What an honor is this rest. It is called the purchased possession because Christ bought it for us with His sacrifice. As we write down the price our purchases cost us, so let us write down the price of heaven as—*The Precious Blood of Christ*.

It was costly for Christ, but *Free* for us. If both the Father and the Son freely offer us the purchased life on our willing acceptance; and if they freely send the Holy Spirit to enable us to accept; what do we have in heaven that is not free? O the everlasting admiration that must surprise the saints to think of this freeness! What an astonishing thought it will be to think of the immeasurable difference between our deservings and receivings—between the state we should have been in, and the state we are in. What depths of gratitude will we feel to look down upon hell and think, "Yonder is the place that sin would have brought me; but this is where Christ has brought me! Yonder lies the wages of my sin, but this eternal life is the gift of God, through Jesus Christ my Lord. [Rom. 3:23-24] Who made the difference? Would I not now have been in hell if I had had my own way, and been allowed my own will? Would I not have lingered in Sodom until the flames had ignited me, if God had not in mercy brought me out?" We know to whom the praise is due and shall be given forever.

Let "Deserved" be written on the door of hell; but on the door of heaven, "The Free Gift."

Special mercy arouses more gratitude than universal mercy. If Pharaoh had passed as safely as Israel through the Red Sea, the miracle would have been less memorable. If the rest of the world had not been drowned, the saving of Noah had not been so noteworthy. If Sodom and Gomorrah had not burned, the deliverance of Lot would not have been talked of so much. That will surely be a day to remember, when there shall be two in one bed, and two in the field, the one taken and the other left (Luke 17:34, 36).

We will enjoy the communion of saints. As we have been together in duty, danger, and distress, so shall we be together in the great deliverance. If the forethought of sitting down with Abraham and Isaac and Jacob in the kingdom of heaven may be our proper joy, how much more the real sight and actual experience? It is surely comforting to think of that day when we shall join with Moses in his song, with David in his psalms of praise, and with all the redeemed in the song of the Lamb forever. [Rev. 5:9-13]

Not only our old acquaintances, but all the saints of all ages, whose faces in the flesh we never saw, we shall there both know and enjoy. Yes, even angels, as well as saints, will be our acquaintances. Those angels, who now are willingly helping us, as God's invisible agents, will then be our companions in joy. It is a beautiful characteristic of the heavenly rest, that we are "fellow citizens with the saints, and of the household of God" (Eph. 2:19). . . .

He who makes His people "like a tree planted by the rivers of water, who brings forth his fruit in his season" (Ps. 1:3), will also give them the reward in His season. Do we complain because we do not find a Canaan in the wilderness? Do we lament because we cannot sing the Lord's song in a strange land? (Ps. 137:4). Do we groan because we find no harbor in the middle of the ocean? Do we object because we cannot sleep during working-hours? Wouldn't all of these things be very unseasonable? Shall we then wonder why we cannot have heaven on earth? Wouldn't that be just as unseasonable?

The new nature which God gives the redeemed, matches the reward that awaits them. Indeed, their holiness is provided by the Spirit of Christ to fit them for heaven. God provides a spiritual rest suitable to their spiritual nature.

We are now as the fish in an aquarium. There is enough water in the aquarium to keep the fish alive, but what is that compared with the ocean? In heaven we shall live in a compatible environment. Christian, this is a rest after your own heart; it contains all that your heart could desire. That which you long for, pray for, work for; there you shall find it all.

Worth Thinking About

All of us need to ponder the fact that our fellowship with God the Father is through the merit of the perfect Son of God, Jesus Christ. The gift and the power of God is far greater than any of our many failings. Thus, all our rejoicing in the heavenly rest will be in honor of the Lamb that was slain before the world ever began.

PRAISE THE LORD IN HEAVENLY PLACES

Praise His Name with praise unending, for His Name alone is great;

Over heaven and earth exalted reigns the Lord in kingly state.

He has greatly blessed His people. Therefore, all ye saints give praise;

Chosen of the Lord and precious, thankful hallelujahs raise.

—Anonymous

Prayer

DEAR FATHER, OUR DEBT TO YOU DOES NOT MAKE US NEEDY; RATHER WHAT WE OWE HAS MADE US RICH IN THAT YOU GIVE US THE BLESSINGS OF HEAVEN THAT WE MIGHT REST IN YOUR WORK. THANK YOU THAT IT HAS PLEASED YOU TO GIVE US MORE THAN WE COULD EVER IMAGINE OR ASK FOR. AMEN.

WHAT ARE WE TO MAKE OF "NEAR DEATH" EXPERIENCES?

Erwin Lutzer

Pastor Erwin Lutzer of The Moody Church of Chicago provides a word of warning about reading too much into near-death experiences. Lutzer, who has a Master's Degree in philosophy from Loyola University, feels great Christian discernment is called for in such matters. All claims about having visited heaven need to be measured against what the Bible says. Here in this excerpt from his book, *One Minute After You Die*, from Moody Publishers in 2007, Lutzer sorts out how to evaluate near-death claims.

⸺⸺

What do these experiences prove? Apparently, they do confirm that at death the soul separates from the body. A few patients not only looked back and saw doctors hover around their body, but could see what was going on in other places in the hospital. This, it seems, is impossible unless the soul had actually left the body and could review earth from a different perspective.

We have reason to believe that a person may see Christ in the twilight zone between life and death. Before Stephen was stoned God gave him a glimpse into heaven. Stephen said, "Behold, I see the heavens opened up and the Son of Man standing at the right hand of God" (Acts 7:56). This experience was unique in that it happened before Stephen died, not at death. Here was positive encouragement that heaven was waiting to receive him!

The apostle Paul had a similar experience, though some think that he actually died when he was caught up into paradise, where he heard "inexpressible words, which a man is not permitted to speak" (2 Corinthians 12:4). Since he said it happened fourteen years before writing these words to the church at Corinth, there is at least some evidence that the event coincided with his experience at Lystra, where he was stoned and dragged out of the city presumed dead (Acts 14:19-20). If he did die and then revived, this account could be classified as a near-death experience, or perhaps even a "revived from death" experience.

If Stephen saw our Lord before he died, and if Paul died and was caught up into paradise, it is just possible that other believers might also have such a vision. Reports of seeing Christ or relatives long dead might have some validity. We should not expect such experiences, but they could happen.

The problem, of course, is that we cannot accept without scrutiny what people claim to have seen behind the curtain. Near-death experiences may or may not reflect the true conditions of life beyond death. They must be carefully evaluated to see whether they conform to the biblical picture of the hereafter. Also, the prior beliefs of those who report what they have seen and heard are essential in evaluating what was experienced.

Worth Thinking About

Many books about near-death experiences have been best sellers, but they often repeat vague reports of having seen a light at the end of a long tunnel followed by a general feeling of contentment and peace. Few of them talk about experiencing the joy of fellowship with Christ and with others who have known him. Many authors conclude after their experiences that there is life after death, and so people shouldn't worry about death. How does this view differ from the biblical picture of what God has for the believer?

SWALLOWED UP IN VICTORY

For the perishable must clothe itself with the imperishable and the mortal with mortality. When the perishable has been clothed with the imperishable, and the immortal with immortality, then the saying that is written will come true: "Death has been swallowed up in victory."

"Where, O death, is your victory?
Where, O death is your sting?"

The sting of death is sin, and the power of sin is the law. But thanks be to God! He gives us the victory through our Lord Jesus Christ. Therefore, my dear brothers, stand firm. Let nothing move you. Always give yourselves fully to the work of the Lord, because you know that your labor in the Lord is not in vain. (1 Cor. 15:53-58 NIV)

*P*rayer

DEAR FATHER, THOUGH DEATH IS INEVITABLE, HAVING COME BECAUSE OF OUR SEPARATION FROM YOU, IN CHRIST WE HAVE BEEN MADE ALIVE AND WILL LIVE IN HEAVENLY PLACES WITH HIM. THANK YOU FOR THIS ASTONISHING GIFT, WHICH IS THE ANSWER TO YOUR VERY OWN QUESTION: "WHERE, O DEATH IS YOUR STING?" ALL GLORY TO YOU THAT THE STING OF DEATH HAS BEEN REMOVED IN CHRIST. AMEN.

WILL OUR HEAVENLY BODIES BE REAL OR IMMATERIAL?

John A. Schep

Author John A. Schep reminds us that Christians have always taught that our resurrected bodies will come forth in the afterlife as real physical bodies such as Jesus had after his own resurrection: Jesus could eat, he could show his scars, and he could make a meal on a beach. The combination of a real body that is sinless, renewed—and able to dart around heaven and go through walls as Jesus did—expands our concept of the new world we will be living in. The Christian has far more to look forward to than in any other of the world's religions, some of which give little hope to those who die. But our life will be a real life, lived to the fullest. This selection is taken from Dr. Schep's book *The Nature of the Resurrected Body: A Study of the Biblical Data*, published by Wm. B. Eerdmans in 1964.

The future resurrection of deceased believers is the issue upon which Paul focuses. . . . We do not know the positive ground for denying this doctrine among the Corinthians [see 1 Cor. 15:16-58]. As Christians they could not have believed in a total and final destruction of man at death. Rather, in Greek fashion, they must have believed in an after-life for the human soul or spirit and in eternal bliss for the spirits of the believers. This is implied in Paul's statement (v. 18) that if Christ is not raised, then also those that are fallen asleep in Christ have perished. Apparently they did not doubt that their deceased brethren enjoyed a blessed condition. . . .

At any rate, these erring Christians in Corinth denied that there is a resurrection of the dead (literally, of corpses) at the end of the ages.

They must have taken offense at what A. Oepke calls "the materialism of the Jewish hope" and denied, to use the words of Grosheide, "the resurrection of the *flesh*" (KNT). Moffatt finds a parallel in the denial of the resurrection by some Christians a century later, of whom Justin Martyr writes that he heard them declare: "There is no resurrection of the dead, but as soon as we die our souls are taken up in heaven." Justin rejects such teaching as unorthodox: "I and all other Christians of orthodox belief know that there will be a resurrection of the flesh. . . ."

To combat this denial of the resurrection Paul appeals to the resurrection of Christ as he had preached it to the Corinthians and as they had come to believe in it when they were converted . . . as the resurrection of one who was buried and then raised again, i.e., who was raised in the same body as that in which he had died and was buried.

In the light of this resurrection (so Paul argues in vv. 13ff.) it is impossible to deny the resurrection of death men, either because dead human bodies cannot possibly be raised again, or because the human body is not fit to share in the future life. . . .

If Christ is not risen, i.e., if his body is still in the power of death, then he has failed as our representative. Then there is no forgiveness of sins because he did not really atone for sin. Nor is there any victory, in any sense of the word, over death. Then our faith in him is of no avail in this life (v. 17), and there is *no hope for a blessed future* for those that died in faith (v. 18). Without his atoning death and his victorious resurrection Christianity is a complete delusion, because our present as well as our future is decided by what our representative did and underwent.

However, Paul argues, Christ was raised indeed, as even the erring Corinthians know. But then that devastating conception that dead men are not raised is untrue and must be abandoned. One dead man has already been raised from the grave, body and all: Christ, our representative. Therefore as certainly as our relation with Christ guarantee our victory over death: the resurrection of our bodies at Christ's coming (vv. 20-23). . . .

This does not exclude the fact that this resurrection will cause a great change in the body, as is clear both from what Scripture teaches concerning the resurrection-body of Christ and from Paul's own teachings in the second part of 1 Corinthians 15.

---

*W*orth Thinking About

Although we know that to be absent from the body is to be present with the Lord (see Phil 1:21-24), it is important to realize that our ultimate destiny is to live as resurrected men and women in Christ's kingdom. God created perfect bodies for Adam and Eve in the beginning, and in the end we will all have perfect bodies in our eternal glory that are somehow our old bodies now transformed by our resurrection. Do you have trouble identifying with a sinless physical body? Does the promise of having such a body make our promised future more real to you? We will live eternally in a body that, we are promised, will be "like unto his glorious body." Perhaps this new state of our bodies in heaven has the most meaning for those of us who have crippling disabilities now. A healthy person hardly ever thinks of his or her body at all—and is probably not necessarily looking forward to a new body. Yet God has left no one out of his plans for the world to come. The blind, the injured, the deaf will be utterly transformed. And those who aren't happy, in some way, with their bodies now will find no fault with their new bodies in heaven.

CLOTHED WITH OUR HEAVENLY DWELLING

Now we know that if the earthly tent we live in is destroyed, we have a building from God, an eternal house in heaven, not built by human hands. Meanwhile we groan, longing to be clothed with our heavenly dwelling, because when we are clothed, we will not be found naked. For while we are in this tent, we groan and are burdened, because we do not wish to be unclothed but to be clothed with our heavenly dwelling, so that what is mortal may be swallowed up by life. Now it is God who has made us for this very purpose and has given us the Spirit as a deposit, guaranteeing what is to come.

Therefore we are always confident and know that as long as we are at home in the body we are away from the Lord. We live by faith, not by sight. We are confidant, I say, and would prefer to be away from the body and at home with the Lord.—2 Corinthians 5:1-5 NIV

*P*rayer

DEAR FATHER, THANK YOU FOR THE NEW BODIES WE WILL HAVE AT THE DAY OF RESURRECTION WHEN ALL YOUR CHILDREN WILL BE GATHERED FOR THE "MARRIAGE SUPPER OF THE LAMB" (REV. 19:7). JUST AS OUR HUMAN FLESH IS REAL AND SENSIBLE TO OUR TOUCH SO MAY OUR FAITH IN A PHYSICAL RESURRECTION BE REAL. AMEN.

How Will Heaven Be Similar to Life Now?

John MacArthur

Most commentators these days are coming to the conclusion that our home in the new heavens and new earth will be much like what we experience now, only we and the new creation will be without sin and full of the first promise that lay before Adam and Eve. God's original plan for earth certainly wasn't bad; it simply wasn't followed. Human activity guided by love for one another will make all things new but strangely familiar, as though we discover our own best selves and best earth for the first time. This thought is emphasized by Dr. John MacArthur in *The Glory of Heaven: The Truth About Heaven, Angels, and Eternal Life,* revised from an earlier version and published by Crossway in 2012.

⸺∞⸺

The apostle [Paul] lists several of the things that are passing away [from earth]; marriage, weeping, earthly rejoicing, and ownership. All the *schëma* of the world is passing away. *Schëma* refers to fashion, manner of life, and a way of doing things. . . .

Paul is not questioning the legitimacy of these earthly blessings such as marriage, normal human emotions, and earthly ownership. But he is saying that we must never allow our emotions and possessions to control us so that we become entangled by this passing world. . . .

If you are already married . . . this does not mean you should become indifferent to your marriage. Too much elsewhere in

Scripture elevates the importance of marriage and commands husbands and wives to seek to honor God through the marriage relationship. . . . While married couples are heirs together of the grace of *this* life (1 Peter 3:7), the institution of marriage is passing away. There are higher eternal values. . . .

The New Testament indicates even more clearly that our identities will remain unchanged. While sharing the Passover meal with his disciples, Christ said, "Take this [cup], and divide it among yourselves. For I tell you that from now on I will not drink of the fruit of the vine until the kingdom of God comes" (Luke 22:17-18). Christ was promising that he and his disciples *would* drink the fruit of the vine together again—in heaven. Elsewhere Jesus makes a similar, but even more definite, promise: "I tell you, many will come from east and west and recline at table with Abraham, Isaac, and Jacob in the kingdom of heaven" (Matthew 8:11). . . .

In heaven we will all be one loving family. The immense size of the family will not matter in the infinite perfection of heaven. There will be ample opportunity for close relationships with everyone, and our eternity will be spent in just that kind of rich, unending fellowship.

Describing the Lord's appearing and the resurrection of the saints who have died, Paul writes, "we who are alive, who are left, will be caught up *together with them* in the clouds to meet the Lord in the air, and so we will always be *with the Lord*" (1 Thessalonians 4:17). Paul's purpose in writings was to comfort some of the Thessalonians who evidently thought their dying loved ones would miss the return of Christ and that they would then be separated from them forever. Paul says in verse 18, "Encourage one another with these words. . . ." Paul's promise that we will all be "together with them [and with] the Lord" forever implies that we shall renew fellowship with every redeemed person whom we have known. . . .

If you're worried about feeling out of place in heaven, don't. Heaven will seem more like home than the dearest spot on earth to you. It is uniquely designed by a tender, loving Savior to be the place where we will live together for all eternity and enjoy him forever—in the fullness of our glorified humanity.

Worth Thinking About

In the beginning God created everything and declared it good. Have you ever tried to ponder what a truly good world would be like and feel like and what satisfactions it will hold? If so inclined, and as an exercise for your imagination, you might try sitting down and writing out your own ideas of what it will be like to live in a world restored from the fall. It could be very much like the earth we have now, only an earth perfect in every way.

MADE IN THE IMAGE OF GOD

So God created man in His own image, in the image of God He created him; male and female He created them. Then God blessed them, and God said to them, "Be fruitful and multiply; fill the earth and subdue it; have dominion over the fish of the sea, over the birds of the air, and over every living thing that moves on the earth. . . ."

Then God saw everything that He had made, and it was very good.—Gen. 1:27-28, 31.

Prayer

DEAR FATHER, HELP US TO UNDERSTAND WHY LOVE FOR OTHERS IS SO IMPORTANT AND THAT BY LOVING OTHERS WE DON'T JUST LOVE OURSELVES BUT YOU. GRANT US AN ABSORPTION IN THE WONDER OF OTHER PEOPLE AND THE AMAZING FELLOWSHIP WE CAN HAVE IN CHRIST. AMEN.

WHAT CAN A CHILD TEACH US ABOUT HEAVEN?

George MacDonald (1824-1905)

George MacDonald was a prolific writer and preacher, who influenced a diverse group of writers. Mark Twain, Madeline L 'Engle, G. K. Chesterton, and W. H. Auden all claim to have been influenced by this Presbyterian mystic—not a comfortable thing to be in the Scotland of his day. Because he thought 'outside the box,' when he had an insight, it was a keen one. C. S. Lewis credited MacDonald with "baptizing his imagination" and for showing him how the supernatural might operate in the real world in the book *Phantastes*. Others find the same book a complete puzzle. What do you think of MacDonald's views on the childlikeness of heaven? What does it even mean to be childlike?

⎯⎯∞⎯⎯

To receive a child in the name of Jesus is to receive Jesus; to receive Jesus is to receive God; therefore to receive the child is to receive God himself.

That such is the feeling of the words [of Christ that instruct us to be great in the kingdom of heaven by becoming like a little child; Matt. 18:4—Ed.], and that such was the feeling in the heart of our Lord when he spoke them, I may show from another golden thread that may be traced through the shining web of his golden words.

What is the kingdom of Christ? A rule of love, of truth—a rule of service. The king is the chief servant in it. "The kings of the earth have dominion: it shall not be so among you." [Mark 10:43] "The Son of Man came to minister." [Matt. 20:28] "My Father worketh hitherto, and I work." [John 5:17] The great Workman is the great King, labouring for his own. So he that would be greatest among them, and come nearest to the King himself, must be the servant of all. It is *like king like subject* in the kingdom of heaven. No rule of force, as of one kind over another kind. It is the rule of *kind,* of nature, of deepest nature—of *God.*

If, then, to enter into this kingdom, we must become children, the spirit of children must be its pervading spirit throughout, from lowly subject to lowliest king. The lesson added by St. Luke to the presentation of the child is: "For he that is least among you all, the same shall be great." [Luke 9:48] And Matthew says: "Whosoever shall humble himself as this little child, the same is greatest in the kingdom of heaven." [Matt. 18:4]

Hence the sign that passes between king and subject. The subject kneels in homage to the kings of the earth: the heavenly king takes his subject in his arms. This is the sign of the kingdom between them. This is the all-pervading relation of the kingdom. . . .

To receive the child because God receives it, or for its humanity, is one thing; to receive it because it is like God, or for its childhood, is another. The former will do little to destroy ambition. Alone it might argue only a wider scope to it, because it admits all men to the arena of the strife. But the latter strikes at the very root of emulation. As soon as even service is done for the honour and not for the service-sake, the doer is that moment outside the kingdom.

But when we receive the child in the name of Christ, the very childhood that we receive to our arms is humanity. We love its humanity in its childhood, for childhood is the deepest heart of humanity—its divine heart; and so in the name of the child we receive all humanity. Therefore, although the lesson is not about humanity, but about childhood, it returns upon our race, and we receive our race with wider arms and deeper heart. . . .

If there is in heaven a picture of that wonderful teaching, doubtless we shall see represented in it a dim childhood shining from the faces of all that group of disciples of which the centre is the Son of God with a child in his arms. The childhood, dim in the faces of the men, must be shining trustfully clear in the face of the child.

But in the face of the Lord himself, the childhood will be triumphant—all his wisdom, all his truth upholding that radiant serenity of faith in his father.

Worth Thinking About

How were the apostles childlike in the way they behaved? What is to be praised in having a childlike attitude toward God? Why does wishing to be great in the kingdom of heaven make that person small and ill-fitted for greatness? How would a childlike attitude cause one to be considered great in the kingdom?

FORWARD THROUGH THE AGES

Forward thro' the ages in unbroken line,
Move the faithful spirits at the call divine;
Gifts in diff'ring measure, hearts of one accord,
Manifold the service, one the sure reward.
Forward thro' the ages in unbroken line,
Move the faithful spirits at the call divine.

—Frederick L. Hosmer

Prayer

DEAR FATHER, HUMBLE US THAT WE MIGHT BECOME LIKE LITTLE CHILDREN, CHILDLIKE IN OUR FAITH AND TRUSTING IN YOU THE WAY WE WOULD TRUST A FAITHFUL PARENT. TEACH US HOW TO PLACE THE MYSTERIES OF LIFE INTO YOUR HANDS AND FOCUS ON LIVING WITH WHAT WE DO UNDERSTAND. AMEN.

What Can the Sermon on the Mount Tell Us About Heaven?

E. M. Bounds (1835-1913)

Edward McKendree Bounds was a noted man of prayer. Prayer was this Methodist Pastor's spiritual specialty; and his books on prayer are considered devotional classics, even if they are a bit challenging. Bounds developed the habit of waking at four in the morning to pray for three hours every day. Many attested to his habits, avowing there was power in the praying. Bounds is also noted for his small book *Heaven: A Place, A City, A Home.* Here he explains why God's command that we be "perfect" is only to be expected of those whose ultimate home is heaven. Although the journey may seem long, there is comfort in knowing there is a faithful companion all the way who perfects us.

∞∞∞

[The] sermon on the mount—among His first utterances, if not the very first—begins with heaven. He teaches us to let our light shine that we may glorify our Father in heaven; that except our righteousness exceed the righteousness of the scribes and Pharisees we shall in no case enter into the kingdom of heaven. So He begins His divine mission and marvelous career with heaven accepted, recognized as a matter of course, in full force and to the front.

His first preaching was saturated with the idea of the principles of heaven. "Repent," He said, "for the kingdom of heaven is at hand." The first foundation stone of spiritual character is cemented, impregnated with the same. The first utterance of His first sermon is a beatitude of the kingdom of heaven. The diamond of all diamonds of character is, "Blessed are the pure in heart for they shall see God."

That includes, seeing, knowing, and loving God, but it includes and finds its full realization in heaven. To see God, to see Him in everything, in every tear that dims the eye or breaks the heart—that is heaven, heaven begun on earth. To see God—that is heaven, the highest heaven, heaven to all eternity. "For now we see through a glass, darkly; but then face to face: now I know in part; but then shall I know even as also I am known" (1 Cor. 13:12). He brings us into the presence of the children and their character, and we see the child's inheritance, "if children then heirs." "Blessed are the peacemakers; for they shall be called children of God" (Matt. 5:9).

This leads the way to the last: "Blessed are they which are persecuted for righteousness' sake: for theirs is the kingdom of heaven." "Blessed are ye, when men shall revile you, and persecute you, and shall say all manner of evil against you falsely, for my sake. Rejoice, and be exceedingly glad: for great is your reward in heaven, for so persecuted they the prophets which were before you" (Matt. 5:10-12).

Jesus at the very beginning and in His first call to discipleship stimulates and connects that call with all the alluring weight, comfort, and hope of heaven. Heaven is at the foundation of the system of Jesus, its first thought, brightest hope, strongest faith. Their Father, He tells them, is in heaven, a place worthy the abode of God, and they must so demean themselves as to reflect glory on their Father in heaven.

The righteousness of His followers must exceed the righteousness of the Scribes and Pharisees, else the glories of heaven would never be theirs. . . . The Father's character must be the children's character, the Father's conduct, the children's conduct, the Father's place, the children's place, the Father's home, the children's home.

"Ye have heard that it hath been said, Thou shalt love thy neighbor, and hate thine enemy. But I say unto you, love your enemies, bless them that curse you, do good to them that hate you, and pray for them which despitefully use you, and persecute you; that ye may be the children of your Father which is in heaven, for he maketh his sun to rise on the evil and the good, and sendeth his rain on the just and the unjust. For if ye love them which love you, what reward have ye? do not even the publicans the same? And if ye salute your brethren only, what do ye more than others? Do not even the publicans so? Be ye therefore perfect, even as your Father which is in heaven is perfect" (Matt. 5:43-48).

Worth Thinking About

Let us be clear: life is full of pitfalls, mistakes, and downright wrongdoing, on a daily basis. Yet we are called upon to be perfect even as our Father in heaven is perfect. How can that be? Do our attitudes really have to match up with our actions? Is holding hatred in my heart really as bad as being a literal murderer? What does Jesus mean when he says our righteousness must exceed that of the Pharisees? Why should we start the journey of being made perfect now when we know God will fully complete the job in heaven? What part does grace play in all of this?

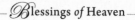
I WALK WITH THE KING

O soul near despair in the lowlands of strife,

Look up and let Jesus come into your life;

The joy of salvation to you He would bring—

Come into the sunlight and walk with the King.

I walk with the King, hallelujah! I walk with the King, praise His name!

No longer I roam, my soul faces home, I walk and I talk with the
King.—James Rowe

Prayer

DEAR FATHER, THANK YOU FOR YOUR WORK IN OUR LIVES, THAT YOU ARE FITTING US FOR HEAVEN, AND THAT WE WILL BE MADE PERFECT AT THE LAST DAY. IN THE MEANWHILE, AS WE JOURNEY ON IN THIS LIFE, ENCOURAGE OUR HEARTS TO THINK THAT, ALTHOUGH THERE ARE STRUGGLES HERE, THERE WILL BE JOY IN THE END. AMEN.

IS THERE ANY HEAVENLY GOOD IN KEEPING SCORE OF GOOD DEEDS?

Michael Allen Rogers

Dr. Michael Rogers ministers to the Westminster Presbyterian Church of Lancaster, Pennsylvania, and his book—*What Happens After I Die?*, published by Crossway in 2013—comes out of a sermon series he delivered over a period of 26 weeks to his congregation. In this excerpt, Rogers takes up the matter of heavenly rewards for our deeds done here on earth. If you have ever wondered how free salvation works in conjunction with rewards in heaven, perhaps Dr. Roger's comments may provide some insight for you.

We all possess a baseline commercial attitude for estimating the good that we imagine our lives contribute to the world. Since we pay cash for goods and services, and since we consume and are paid by the hour or week to labor for an employer, it comes naturally to our mercenary minds that good deeds, acts of kindness, charitable giving, spiritual faithfulness, or even having more sheep in your congregation's corral should somehow be paid back in spiritual economics.

If my neighbor uses his snowblower to open the drifts across the mouth of my driveway, should I ask my wife to bake him a pie as a gift—or is it enough for me to verbally thank him and leave it at that? If I am the one using the snowblower for the same kindly deed, do I quietly watch to see if there will be recompense forthcoming from my neighbor, yet act surprised when it is given? We are truly devious creatures as we keep score in these matters.

Jesus told Peter that all who sacrifice any tangible benefit in this life for his sake, whether wife, family, or real estate will receive "a hundredfold" back, and inherit eternal life as well (Matt. 19:29). This is an indication of definite future rewards. . . .

Immediately after Peter's inquiry about rewards, Matthew 20:1-16 presents the parable of workers in the vineyard. There Jesus taught about the workers hired at different times for day labor in the fields, with all being paid the same wage at sundown. Those who worked all day had at first agreed to the wage, so it was fair for them. For those who worked only the last two hours of the afternoon, the same wage was super fair. No one was cheated. This employer's action obviously demonstrated God's abundant grace: one and the same salvation is experienced in equal measure by a first-century apostle of Jesus like Peter and by the lowliest believer in the twenty-first century; there is a fundamental equality at the base of our salvation. "For by grace you have been saved through faith. And this is not your own doing; it is the gift of God, not a result of works, so that no one may boast," declares Ephesians 2:8-9.

No human being who enters God's final dwelling in the new heaven and the new earth will dare say, "Thank goodness I was found worthy." Perish the idea! All who are redeemed in Jesus Christ are equally redeemed. In terms of salvation, all believers receive one identical crown of grace as God's free gift.

If you must think of salvation in terms of rewards, consider it as a portion of the prize God the Father gave Jesus the Son for his perfect obedience unto death. Isaiah 53 predicted that the will of the Lord will prosper in Jesus's death and resurrection. God predicted of his Son, "Therefore I will divide him [Christ] a portion with the many, and he shall divide the spoil with the strong, because he poured out his soul to death and was numbered with the transgressors" (v. 12). The kingdom of heaven is God's reward given to Jesus. He shares it by sheer grace with all who believe on his name. He is the general after a great victory, parceling out spoils from the vanquished army among his loyal troops.

Worth Thinking About

The struggle to serve God for his glory and not our own is complicated. Think of the times you have done good deeds but had them treated as nothing by the person who received them. How did you feel? Clearly Scripture teaches that good deeds will be rewarded, but Scripture also teaches that "it is God who works in you to will and to act according to His good pleasure" (Phil. 2:13). How can God reward what he is already motivating us to do? Perhaps like all mysteries that arise out of the divine will, we must wait until heaven appears to find out.

THE SPIRIT SEARCHES ... THE DEEP THINGS OF GOD

"Eye has not seen, nor ear heard,

Nor have entered into the heart of man

The things which God has prepared for those who love Him."

But God has revealed them to us through His spirit. For the Spirit searches all things, yes, the deep things of God.

—1 Corinthians 2:9

Prayer

DEAR FATHER, THANK YOU THAT YOU ARE DETERMINED TO POUR OUT THE VERY BLESSINGS OF HEAVEN UPON US AND THAT ALL WHO SERVE YOU WILL BE SATISFIED THAT YOU HAVE TREATED THEM FAIRLY. HELP US TO BE EARNEST IN OUR WORK AND TO KNOW THAT ANY REWARD IN HEAVEN WILL BE GENEROUS BEYOND OUR WILDEST DREAMS. AMEN.

How Old Will We Be in Heaven?

Peter Kreeft

Naturally, we are curious about this matter of our age in heaven. It seems unlikely to us that everyone would be at the age they died. This concept would leave some exceedingly young and others exceedingly old and competing for the prize of being the oldest person there: undoubtedly Methuselah. Still philosophical theologians are not afraid to take a stab at an answer. Even St. Thomas Aquinas got into the imaginative act, as Peter Kreeft relates in his book *Everything You Ever Wanted to Know About Heaven. . . But Never Dreamed of Asking.* If a child asked you such a question, how would you answer it? It would not be unusual for a child to expect a parent to have a believable answer!

As heavenly bodies do not die, they do not age. So what age will we be in Heaven?

Resuscitated patients report their out-of-the-body body as not having any particular age. Naturally; it is measured not by *chronos* but only by *kairos,* not by physical time but by soul time. And since time is differently related to the soul and the soul differently related to the body in Heaven, therefore time is differently related to the body in Heaven. The measure of matter moving through space does not measure Heavenly bodies; "the heavenly bodies" do not measure our Heavenly bodies.

We see traces of Heavenly agelessness on earth occasionally: in the timeless wisdom of the infant or in the womblike stillness of the wise who approach death in perfect peace. This agelessness is like the perfect age that includes all ages, as all ages of one's life pass in instant review before the dying. The Heavenly age is no age and all ages.

Saint Thomas Aquinas taught that the perfect age was thirty-three, since it was the age Christ had attained when He died; therefore, he thought everyone would have a body like a thirty-three-year-old body in Heaven. . . . [T]his is to be taken only symbolically, not literally, because in Heaven there is neither birth nor death, the measuring sticks of age.

Worth Thinking About

Of course, there is so much we don't know about heaven, our curiosity outruns our evidence. Thus, by faith we must leave certain questions in the hands of the Father, the Son, and the Holy Spirit. We know so much, but we always want to know more. Perhaps part of the joy in looking forward to heaven is in knowing that it will be good to be there and letting that truth suffice for us. God will take care of such things as the appropriate age for those who died in their youth or for those who died at 110. Still, it is fun to speculate, as others have done. What age would you want to be in heaven? Can you imagine feeling all your favorite moments of different ages at the same time?

PRAISE THE LORD IN HEAVENLY PLACES

Praise His Name with praise unending, for His Name alone is great;
Over heaven and earth exalted reigns the Lord in kingly state.
He has greatly blessed His people. Therefore, all ye saints give praise;
Chosen of the Lord and precious, thankful hallelujahs raise.

—Anonymous

rayer

DEAR FATHER, IT REMAINS FOR US TO SEE WHAT THE ACTUAL SPECIFICS OF HEAVEN MAY BE, BUT HELP US TO GROW IN TRUST THAT ALL MANNER OF THINGS WILL BE JUST RIGHT IN HEAVEN AND THAT PERFECT PEACE WILL FILL OUR HEARTS (SEE MARK 7:37). AMEN.